Strength in the Struggle

STRENGTH IN THE
Struggle

Leadership

Development for Women

VASHTI MURPHY MCKENZIE

The Pilgrim Press
Cleveland

In memory of pioneering leaders who happen to be women

Ida Murphy Peters
Vashti Turley Murphy
Martha Elizabeth Murphy
Frances Murphy I
Elizabeth Murphy Moss

and those who continue to make history

Carlita Murphy Jones
Frances Murphy II

The Pilgrim Press, 700 Prospect Avenue, Cleveland, Ohio 44115-1100
www.pilgrimpress.com
© 2001 by Vashti Murphy McKenzie
Unless otherwise noted, all scripture quotations are from the New Revised Standard Version of the Bible, © 1989 by the Division of Christian Education of the National Council of the Churches of Christ in the U.S.A., and are used by permission. Occasional adaptations have been made for clarity and inclusiveness.
All rights reserved. Published 2001
Printed in the United States of America on acid-free paper
06 05 04 03 02   5 4 3 2

Library of Congress Cataloging-in-Publication Data

McKenzie, Vashti M., 1947–
    Strength in the struggle : leadership development for women /
  Vashti Murphy McKenzie.
       p.   cm.
    ISBN 0-8298-1212-1 (alk. paper)
    1. Afro-American women clergy—Training of.   2. Christian
leadership.   I. Title.

BR563.N4 M354   2001
253'.082—dc21

                                                        2001034352

Contents

๛

Preface

༄

MY FIRST BOOK, *Not without a Struggle,* was a labor of love. The gestation period covered several decades, but it only took three years to deliver the offspring. The baby was eagerly received and went into its second printing in less than one week. The publisher and the parent were both relieved.

Strength in the Struggle is a continuum of *Not without a Struggle.* It continues my wrestle with leadership because there is not a preponderance of leadership material for women who seek to work effectively and efficiently.

Strength in the Struggle is a potpourri of leadership information. A potpourri is a miscellany—a mixture of diverse substances blended together to create a new entity. A potpourri of flowers creates a fragrant blend of many scents.

The book is designed to create a fragrant bouquet of lessons to give confidence to leaders who serve in the best of circumstances and those who need support in hostile environments. It provides encouragement and support for leaders who happen to be women. *Strength in the Struggle* is a potpourri of sermons, wisdom, "tidbits," and quotes to help you find the answers that strengthen your leadership. It also includes insight and interviews with a group of women from diverse fields who share the blessings and burden of leadership.

The sermons are presented in the oral stylization of their original presentation. The insight and interviews are interspersed with reflections of my own leadership journey from a newspaper's city desk to the first women elected and consecrated a bishop in the two hundred-and-fourteen-year history of the African Methodist Episcopal Church.

Chapter 1, "A Foundation for Leadership," gives a brief overview of the evolution of leadership thought. It includes the sermon "We're on Our Way Somewhere" that looks at three things that every leader should have: a sense of purpose, high standards and sacrifice.

Chapter 2 is entitled "Experiences Shape Us." Experiences may or may not make or break a leader but they do have impact upon leadership development.

Chapter 3, "Defining Moments," discusses those extraordinary experiences that have the power to change lives forever. Included in this chapter is a unique section, "Dorothy on Leadership." This is a series of lessons, "Dorothy's Leadership Lessons," based on the century-old children's classic by L. Frank Baum, *The Wonderful Wizard of Oz*.

Chapter 4 is "Surviving the Jungle." It is a jungle out there and in order to make it, one must "outwit, outplay, and outlast." Three sermons feature the prophet Nehemiah's method of surviving in the jungle.

Chapter 5 is "Living beyond the Stereotypes." We all have stereotypes that threaten to define who we are and what we can do. The sermon is about Jesus, a Jewish carpenter from Nazareth. It is a place not known for producing good things.

Chapter 6 is "When Someone Needs Help." There are many ways to support other leaders. One way is to mentor them. This chapter includes the "Mentoring of Moses" and "Jethro's Six Steps" to mentoring. Another way is through intercessory prayer. The sermon "I Got Your Back" shows the power of intercessory prayer.

Chapter 7 is "Taking Care of Business." There is nothing like a woman who knows how to take care of business. Two sermons, "Armed and Dangerous," and "Participate in Your Own Rescue," look at two leaders who take two different approaches to the problems they faced. The book ends with a concluding thought.

It is desired that you keep this potpourri as a sweet reminder and bouquet of encouragement for those moments when leadership is more like a burden than a blessing. Share it with others in a group as motivation to explore your own leadership journeys.

Any endeavor undertaken requires the efforts of many people. I want to express my deep appreciation to those who contributed to this body of material. The women who responded to the surveys; the women who shared their leader-stories and wisdom; and the women whose exemplary leadership continues to inspire us all.

I am grateful to the congregations who listened to the genesis of these sermons over the years, especially Payne Memorial African Methodist Episcopal Church. Their love and kindness nurtured me from the pastoral to the Episcopal ministry.

To Cajetta Stephens, Gwen Travis, and Kim Bedford, who type and edit even my handwritten copy—which is a miracle in itself.

Kim Sadler, my editor, is a great encourager. When I thought this would never be finished, she continued to support me. Thank you for your patience and your pushing.

To my sister friends who have prayed me through; Dr. Cecelia Williams Bryant, Dr. Carolyn Showell, Dr. Leah White, and Dr. Peggy Wall.

I am indebted to those who shared their expertise and knowledge through the years. Some of their names and references have long been forgotten, but their seeds of leadership planted in my life are beginning to bear fruit.

I am eternally grateful to a family who share me with the world. My son, Jon, and daughters, Vashti-Jasmine and Joi Marie, have heard all of these things before it was preached. Love and appreciation to my husband Stan, who believed in me before I could see what God was doing in me.

My sisters, "Daughters of Thunder," your imagination will determine how far you go and how high you climb. "Your gifts will make room for you." Leader women, the world is anxious for the exceptional uniqueness you have to offer!

Chapter one

A Foundation for Leadership

꿎

THE STRUGGLE CONTINUES for leaders who happen to be women. They must struggle through a sea of stereotypes to rise to the top of their professions. They must work under glass ceilings, stained, colored or clear, watching what goes on at the top but never reaching the pinnacle themselves.

Leaders who happen to be women had to transform negative barriers into stepping-stones of success. They have had to seize knowledge and opportunities in areas forbidden to them for generations. Many times they serve in isolation. Friends do not understand the demands of their position. Family may not be willing to share them with the world. Peers, who can offer collegiality, are few and far between. They have had to rise, like yeast in baking bread, or steam from a hot cup of tea, sacrificing personal happiness.

Leaders who happen to be women have had to endure the pressure of "stepping out of place" into the forbidden territory of power and authority. Power in the hands of a woman seems to be a frightening reality to many people. Women have often trained less-qualified persons who ascend up the corporate ladder ahead of them. They labor for less pay and reap fewer rewards. A recent quote in a women's magazine indicated that women in the United States earn only seventy-two cents for every dollar earned by men. Women do two-thirds of the work in the world but only receive five percent of the world's income.[1]

Patricia Reid-Merritt notes that women move up in their careers to solve problems others deem hopeless. She quotes one leader, as saying that the only way a woman becomes mayor of a city is if it is bankrupt. Women are given the opportunity to be captain of the ship if it is sinking.[2]

In spite of achievements in the fields of politics, business, arts and entertainment, religion and sports, leaders who are women are still vulnerable. The demise of affirmative action closes important doors to them. Racism presents a continued insurmountable obstacle to overcome. Yet, women have not given up their press for the leadership roles of their dreams. They still have a clear agenda for change and keep the vision of strong, competent leadership before them.

Many women are wearied by the struggle. They become bitter from the experience just doing what their talent demands. To ease the pain of the struggle, we'll begin by first understanding what is a leader, discuss the evolution of leadership thought, and conclude with a sermon "We're on Our Way Somewhere."

LEADERSHIP

Leadership is as simple as tying your shoe. It is initiating a variety of small motor skills working together to achieve a specific task. It is also as complicated as the mathematical equations that spawn the Internet. It is as tricky as extracting seeds from the caverns of a pomegranate. It is as delicate as preserving an orchid outside of a hot house.

Leadership is desired and yet often shunned. It is celebrated and criticized at the same time. It is appreciated and yet despised. It is wanted and yet often exists in hostile environments. Leadership and leaders are admired and sometimes hated.

When leadership flourishes, shaking out the stars of achievement into the air from its tresses of stress and strain, there is an element that rises to destroy its genius. Yet, there is nothing as strong as the courage of exemplary leadership. Leadership is studied, researched, sought after, and touted. The more you know, the more there is to learn about it.

Leadership is also difficult to define. It is a word with several meanings. It is used to refer to those who occupy the role of a leader, as well as to the special traits of those leaders. It is often described as a set of functional responsibilities that must be utilized to maintain an organization's task.[3]

Walter Bennis, leadership guru, indicates that there are three hundred fifty different meanings for leadership.[4] After decades of study and research, no one definition has stood the test of time. He contends that we still are not clear about what separates leadership from non-leadership or effective leaders from noneffective leaders.[5]

John Naisbitt and Patricia Aburdene indicate that leadership includes visioning and expressing new realities and convincing others to embrace and actualize it. It also includes persuading others of the benefits of the new reality.[6]

According to Leighton Ford, earlier studies of leadership examined the qualities or traits that so-called great leaders exerted. Ford sees two factors. There are leaders who take the lead and move people to follow them. He also concludes that any consideration of leadership must include the position of the leaders, plus the process employed and the personality of the leader.[7]

For the purpose of this discussion, leadership is the ability to bring people together for the accomplishment of common goals.[8] It is the process that lends the achieving of those goals with the maintenance of the organization.

THE EVOLUTION OF LEADERSHIP THOUGHT

Leadership appears to have gone through an evolution of thought. Leadership was once thought of as an exclusive right of the privileged. It was then believed that leaders were shaped by events. Today, Stephen Covey and others are promoting the thought of principle-centered leadership. Leadership is not a matter of birth or circumstances, but is driven and shaped by ones belief and values.

When leadership is considered the exclusive right of the privileged, you hear the phrase, "Leaders are born not made." Leadership guided by this thought means that leadership is a matter of birth. You have to be born into the right family or have the right heritage. Leadership is an inherited right. It is born out of a continuum of leader persons who pass the mantle down from one generation to the next. It is like leaders beget leaders. This means that leadership is available to a limited number of people.

Either you are born to it or you are not. If you have, you may lead. If you don't, you follow.

Leadership within this mindset cannot be learned or earned. You cannot aspire to it. There is a major flaw with this thought that leaders are born and not made. The problem is that leadership is not a rare entity limited to a select few. Everyone has the potential within him or her to become a leader. History records the accomplishments of too many women and men who were born outside of privilege at the bottom of the "sugar hills" of the rich and famous.

There is still no simple leadership formula. There may be guides available such as "Seven Steps to Great Leadership" or "Ten Ways to Become a Great Leader," but just following a theoretical formula will not produce a good leader.

Workshops, seminars, and books may help you. They can show you how it is done, but the onus of leadership comes from within you. College can provide you with knowledge but cannot guarantee an education. You can gain knowledge from a book, but the book cannot guarantee wisdom. Once you have learned the theory, it is in the practicum where your skills are honed and tested.

There are leadership experts who considered that there is a fine line between learned behavior and natural ability. Does it really matter how you got it? You may be born with it or you learned it, acquired it, earned it, wished it, stole it, bought it or inherited it from your parental gene pool. One of the myths about leadership is that it is rare like an albino alligator. Another is that it only exists at the top of the economic and social erudite ladder.

Many leaders of great achievements were born of humble beginnings, not in the aristocracy or with any other leaders on the family tree. They were grass roots, no name, often overlooked, and ignored by mainstream society. Yet, they rose to occupy positions of importance, from college presidents, judges, joint chiefs of staff, surgeons, entrepreneurs, record company pioneers, business icons, pastors, and Episcopal leaders.

Mary McCloud Bethune was one black woman with one dream—starting a college where young men and women could receive a good education. She was not born with a silver spoon in her mouth. She was not born at the end of a long line of leaders. Yet in the final analysis, she rose to become a valued member of President Franklin Roosevelt's "kitchen cabinet." The school Bethune-Cookman founded graduated many excellently trained men and women. The thought of leaders "born and not made" gave way to the thought that leaders were made by events. Great leaders were created by great events. Great leaders were ordinary people who were shaped by extraordinary events.

A leader is developed within the midst of challenges and obstacles that face them. It is almost like necessity is the mother of leadership. Events give a person the opportunity to exercise gifts, skills, and talent that would only come into play at that time. Integrity is challenged. Character is molded. Leader style is developed. Vision is sharpened in the event. The ability of moving people towards a common goal is gained not from a birthright, but from the challenge that faced them.

Martin Luther King Jr. was just an ordinary preacher until the Montgomery, Alabama, bus boycott made him a great leader. Merle Evers Williams, former chairwoman of the NAACP, was just an ordinary woman until her husband was violently and suddenly killed. If it had not been for the Philippine's unrest and her husband's death, Corazon Aquino would have been an ordinary woman and not a former, great leader of the island nation.

The thought that trials make leaders gives the impression that anyone can be a leader. If the circumstances are right, anyone can be shaped into a leader. Stephen Covey, author of *Seven Habits of Highly Effective People,* is leading the parade that is taking the thought of leadership one step further. He looks at leadership not based on birth or circumstance, but based upon values or principles. How a leader leads and what a leader does is fueled by the values they hold dear.

John C. Maxwell contends in *The 21 Irrefutable Laws of Leadership* that, no matter what, leadership is leadership.[9] Times, societies, cultures, and technologies will change. The true principles of leadership will be constant in every venue from church to country to community. The leader principles he espouses include "The Law of Process," leadership develops daily, not in a day; "The Law of Navigation," anyone can steer the ship, but it takes a leader to chart the course; "The Law of Solid Ground," trust is the foundation of leadership; "The Law of Respect," leaders naturally follow those who are stronger than themselves; "The Law of Empowerment, only secure leaders give power to others; "The Law of Connection," leaders touch the heart before they touch the hand; and the "Law of Buy-in," people buy into the leader, then the vision.

The evolution of leadership thought has gone through several changes. It began with the idea that "leaders were born, not made." Leadership belonged to a privilege few. It moved on to the idea that necessity was the mother of all leaders. It was the events that made great leaders. Today, it is leadership laws can be learned. What makes a great leader are the principles or core beliefs of a leader.[10]

The Bible relates an occasion in the gospel of Matthew where Jesus was teaching about God's realm. He told a short story about a merchantman who went around looking for goodly pearls. In the telling of the tale are leader principles that would be assets to any leader.

THE WORD

Again, the realm of heaven is like a merchant looking for fine pearls; on finding one pearl of great value, he went and sold all that he had and bought it.—Matthew 13:45–46

We're on Our Way Somewhere

Every leader is going somewhere. Where are you going? Where is your somewhere going? Life is not static or staid; if you refuse to move or forget to move, the world will move on without you. Even when you are not moving, life repositions people and events based on your stagnant location.

Where are you going and where is the somewhere of your going? What is your destination? How long will it take for you to get there? Do you have everything you need for the journey? Are there others riding with you or are you going somewhere by yourself? Leadership requires followers.

Is this the first time you tried to get somewhere? Or is this a return engagement leading others beyond the bottom line, past the status quo, towards the horizon of new realities? Everyone leader should be trying to get somewhere. Somewhere is a lot better than anywhere. Anywhere is where you go when your alternatives are depleted; your choices are limited. After all, any leader can get anywhere. Somewhere is better than anywhere, which is better than nowhere. Nowhere is the easiest destination. If you are going nowhere, nowhere is where you will end up.

Where are you going and where is the somewhere of your going? What do you plan to do when you arrive? You do plan to arrive? Why start out if you do not intend to arrive? What do you plan to do when you get there? What do you plan to do along the way? Have you planned for detours or roadblocks? Every trip is not without incident. Where are you going and where is the somewhere of you going?

Does the journey require preparation? The somewhere where you are going, does it require a prepared mind, a prepared head, a prepared body, a prepared faith? Do you have anyone helping you with the preparation for your somewhere going? Better yet, is there anyone showing you the way? How are you going to get where you are going without someone telling you how to get there or showing you where it is so you can get it yourself.

Are there any books you can read about where you are going? Are there maps that can identify for you the exact location? Are there mentors who can coach you every step of the way? Are there people: family, friends, or peers who stand in the balcony of your life to cheer you on?

These are just simple questions that require complicated answers. Please respond. Where are you going, and where is the somewhere of your going? Every leader should be somewhere. You will not get somewhere living in your comfort zone. You will not get somewhere doing the same things the same way all the time. You will not get somewhere performing unchallenging tasks where no one will bother you, taking no risks, facing few problems, never being concerned about growth or your potential.

Somewhere going requires you to get tired of where you are. Being fed up pushes you to a crucial turning point when enough is enough. Dissatisfaction with a nonproductive plateau compels you to start going somewhere. Where are you going and where is the somewhere of your going? Are you leading in such a way those unswerving, lasting benefits come to you and those who follow you?

Dr. Benjamin Mays, a great African American theologian, writes that what one aspires to tells you about the somewhere of their going. He says he can almost predict their future. What people are really made of are dreams. What one aspires to, what deals beckon, and what interest keeps them moving, indicates their destination.

The Creator has not molded us with aspirations and longings for heights to which we cannot climb, Mays wrote. Look to the horizon, the unattainable calls us to climb new mountains.

Where are you going and where is the somewhere of your going? When life reaches its fullest, it ends all too soon. As soon as you get started, it is time to end. It has hardly begun, and it is soon over. As we pass across the stage of history, we have but one chance to make the best of it. There will be no curtain calls, extra bows or encores. When the curtain goes down on the last act, the theater goes dark. Either you will get somewhere, or you will not make your mark upon the world. It will go unmarked for eons until eternity.

The problem is that so many of us have lived a lifetime going nowhere, settling for less than God intended for us, settling for something less than the best. There is a story often told about two caterpillars enjoying the predictability of their existence. They enjoyed inching along the ground, climbing trees, and feasting on plants. One day, one of the caterpillars wrapped himself up in a cocoon on a branch. The other remained on the ground watching and waiting for his return.

One day he emerged. He dried off his new beautiful wings and began to fly. He marveled at the new things he could do and places he could go. He called to his friend on the ground to join him. "Come on up," he said. "The view is different from up here."

The caterpillar on the ground said, "Looks like too much trouble. You will never get me up in one of those things."

The butterfly flew away. As a leader, you will either have the courage to change and take others with you, or opportunities will fly away.

Leadership has the unique opportunity to create an atmosphere for innovation to take place. Leaders can give permission for advancement to take place. Otherwise, followers may demand it by following those who will. New ideas and new opportunities come to those who decide what they want and have the courage to pursue it. This challenges leaders to have the ability to see potential in everything and everyone.

Matthew presents to us a gathering of the sayings of Christ in orderly segments that forms the basis of inspiration for the early-century church. The life and ministry of Jesus is combined with his ethical teaching. These teachings are grouped into five major discourses, each ending with words similar to "When Jesus had finished saying these things" (Matt. 7:28; 11:1). The evangelist's concern was that readers believe that Jesus is the son of David, the pronounced Messiah of the Hebrews. His own people rejected Jesus. He was crucified as King of the Jews, rose from the grave commissioning disciples to "Go therefore and make disciples of all nations" (Matt. 28:19).

In chapter 13, Matthew is presenting the parables of the realm of heaven. Jesus is a genius instructor. He uses elements common in culture to teach theological concepts. He chooses objects from everyday life as audiovisual aids.

How much faith is needed? If you have faith the size of a tiny mustard seed, you can move mountains. What is the new covenant? The bread, this is my body broken. The wine, this is my blood, shed.

Jesus is teaching about the realm. The realm of heaven, he said, is compared to someone who sowed good seed in his field. But while everybody was asleep, an enemy came and sowed weeds among the wheat and then went away" (Matt. 13: 24–25). The realm of heaven "is like a mustard seed that someone took and sowed in his field" (Matt. 13: 31). The realm of heaven "is like a treasure hidden in a field" (Matt. 13:44). The realm of heaven "is like a net that was thrown into the sea and caught fish of every kind" (Matt. 13: 47).

Our text, Matthew 13:45, is a short rendering about the realm of heaven. "Again, the realm of heaven is like a merchant in search of fine pearls; on finding one pearl of great value, he went and sold all that he had and bought it" (Matt. 13:45–46).

Here is a merchant traveling to identify and secure product— fine pearls. His livelihood depended upon the acquisition of goods to sell. This was not a haphazard attempt to look for just anything. The text says he was looking for fine pearls.

The merchantman had a specific purpose for his traveling. This was intentional deliberate behavior. It was not an accident. This was no chance wandering, no inadvertent journey, no accidental arrival—it was on purpose.

If you are going somewhere you must have a specific purpose in mind. Purpose provides direction and destination. It keeps you from scattering your efforts. It helps you to prioritize your energy and resources. It helps you to be focused especially when the destination is in the distant future.

When things fail to go according to plan and people and machines let you down, purpose will remind of all the reasons you put up with such things. When distractions tempt you to detour from your goals, purpose reminds you of your mission.

Purpose helps you handle the frustrations of the journey. It reminds you of the reason for going through what you go through to acquire fine pearls. Purpose will help you be intentional about your gifts and call.

Purpose produces powers. When sunlight is focused through a magnifying glass power is produced. The glass intensifies the rays of the sun. It can burn through substances and start fires. That is what

Purpose does in a leader's life. It magnifies what you have and concentrates it towards a specific goal.

Jesus says that there was a merchantman looking for fine pearls. You must have high standards if you are going somewhere. The man wasn't seeking just any pearl but fine pearls. He was searching for the best pearls not mediocre pearls. He was looking for quality and would not settle for substandard, poor pearls or fabulous fakes.

Your standards should be high enough so as not to compromise whom you are; not to settle for imitation pearls. High standards may not win you a lot of friends or love from an adoring crowd. High standards will win the respect of others. High standards make you the exception and not the rule. It propels you from the land of the ordinary to the realm of the extraordinary.

What amazes me is that extraordinary people distinguished by ethical and moral standards try so hard to become a member of Ordinary Land. They feel rejected and left out by the citizens of Ordinary Land. Hearts break when the members of Ordinary Land exclude them from social events. They wonder why they are not included in hostile takeovers, skimming profits, telling dirty jokes. They try so hard to fit in and go along, to get along, just so they can be with ordinary people. Get over it! High standards protect you from selling out to the highest bidder.

What some people do not realize is that Ordinary never did like Extraordinary in the first place. It is like trying to marry oil and water. They are doomed to separate. Every leader should be going somewhere. In order to get somewhere, you will need purpose and high standards. Lastly, the journey requires sacrifice.

The text explains that when the merchantman found a pearl of great value, he sold everything he had and bought it. The man was willing to sacrifice the total of his possessions.

Booker T. Washington tells the story of one of his students who was low in funds and about to quit school. The young man came to him to tell him he was dropping out.

Washington asked him a series of questions: "Are you willing to work all day and study all night?"

He answered, "Yes."

"Are you willing to slop hogs in the morning and do Latin at midnight?"

The student said, "Yes."

"Will you walk ten miles to borrow a book because you can't afford to buy one?"

The boy said, "Yes."

"Are you willing to memorize your lessons in class and your homework assignments because you don't have a notebook?"

He said, "Yes."

"Are you willing to be cold in the winter and hot in the summer and go hungry just so you can save the money for tuition, buy paper, and pens?"

He said, "Yes."

"What is five years of sacrifice for a lifetime of gain?" asked Washington. What is the point of going somewhere when you are not willing to do what is necessary to get there. What is the point if you're not willing to sacrifice to get it and sacrifice to keep it.

Sacrifice often requires that we do not go along with the crowds who are waiting for the red dot, deep discount dollar days to be declared. It will require you to say "No" to something so you can say "Yes" to your destiny. The pearl will never cost less than your best. The pearl of great value will never be less than you best effort. It is worth it. Every leader should be going somewhere. It will require that you have a purpose, high standards, and be willing to make the sacrifices to achieve your goals.

What is the point in going somewhere, and when you finally get somewhere, you are not willing to sacrifice to get there—or get somewhere, and you are not willing to sacrifice to stay there? Somewhere often requires not following the crowds who are waiting for dollar day, red dot sales, deep discounts to be declared. The lace will never cost less than your best. The place will never cost less your all. Where are you going? Everyone is going somewhere, so where is the somewhere you are going.

I don't know about you, but I am on my way somewhere. Are you going "Somewhere?"

Chapter two

Experiences Shape Us

ॐ

A PART OF THE EVOLUTION of leadership is the thought that events make leaders as previously discussed in chapter 1. Experiences may or may not produce leaders but they do have an impact upon leadership development. Experiences become the lens through which we view and evaluate information and events. They are the ground from which our values and principles begin to take shape.

Any discussion about leadership and women must include thoughts about women's experiences. Experiences shape us. From our earliest memories to the present time, daily living and challenges that deepen us shape our character. Our losses and gains may increase or decrease our motivation. Experiences teach us to either view the world as a hostile place to be feared, a secure environment, or an adventure to be lived. They can taint our perspectives with fear and prejudices. They also provide a rich reservoir for leaders to drink from.

Veronica Duncanson, the sales and marketing manager for Global Life Assurance Bahamas, Ltd., believes experiences shape us:

> The Duncanson name has its roots in Jamaica, West Indies. It represents people who are generally talented, hardworking, progressive, industrious, and leaders. Knowing your "roots" helps you to know who you are, why you do the things you do, and why you act the way you act. With this knowledge, you are able to chart your course for the future.[1]

The experiential ground for men and women leadership is different. Men, for the most part, derive their models of leader behavior from the military or sports milieu. Historically, women were denied extensive experiences in those areas. However, in recent generations, the number of women participating in team sports or military service has increased.

The impetus for leadership rises for many women far from the gridiron, the baseball diamond, and the battlefield. The motivation and momentum leadership thrust is derived out of their experiences in the home, family, church, or social community.

Patricia Aburdene and John Naisbitt in *Megatrends for Women* indicate that leaders who happen to be women reflect and express values, "women's values," that they were socialized to own.[2]

Motherhood becomes an excellent training experience for leadership. The same skills of pacing, balancing tasks and conflicting competition for attention, guiding, monitoring, managing resources, settling disputes, information sharing, teaching, and organization are transferable to other work environments. It is almost like if you can survive the nursery, you can make it in the world of work outside the home.

Many of the games men and women played during formative years were often different. This was more apparent with older generations. The boys played games that vanquished the enemy. Girls played games based on relationships and mutual activities.

Today the barriers that separate many gender games have come down. Girls play army, cowboys, and Mortal Kombat. Boys play with stuffed "friends" or action figures. Much of leadership development for women found its genesis in traditional experiences assigned to women. It is out of the care-and-nurturing-of-others role that woman developed the leadership skills of encouragement and support.[3]

The traditional male leadership style has been described as transactional. James McGregor Burns and others conclude that this is a leader who relies on giving orders, rank, and limits and defines, is rigid, controls information, and tends to be impersonal. Its foundational bases are military and sports archetypes.[4]

Aburdene and Naisbitt describe women's leadership as encompassing six traits. They are: valuing creativity, empowering others, motivating, inviting speaking out, rewarding versus punishing, and leadership over management.[5] Women tend to be transforming leaders who are inclusive, share power and information, and are boosters of the self-worth of others and their work.

Many women never learned the control and command of the military motif. Women who exercised the hierarchal reward for good performance and punishment for poor production were not always received well. People tend to make the assumption that women lend humanness to their leadership skills. They have the ability to read body language and the meaning behind words and actions and the subtle, interpersonal dexterity to empathize, reach out, empower, network, and facilitate.

Maxwell Gillette says of his wife, Frankie Jacobs Gillette, president and co-owner of G & G Enterprises in San Francisco, California, that her combination of businesswoman and humanitarian serves her and others well.[6]

Leadership rising from "women values" thrives in a societal climate of rampant change. The dot-com information age has broken traditional leadership molds and the lines that separate gender roles have become blurred. Younger generations are less likely to tolerate the demand-and-command leader but look to those who treat them with respect, creating environments where they can grow and flourish.

Stepping into the places of decision, women did not have the traditional experiences to fall in line with traditional modes of leadership. The only wells of experience they had to draw from were home, family, church, and community. Left to their own creative devices, women developed their style derived from their own experiences.

Noel Irwin Hentschel is the eldest of ten children. Her mother was unable to take full responsibility for her children. It was left to Hentschel to fix lunches and check homework. All of her siblings attended Notre Dame Academy. If any of her brothers and sisters fell behind in their work, the principal, Sister Marie Elizabeth, held her accountable.

At the time she felt that the principal did not like her. Now she realizes that the principal was building character. Her early experiences are a rich reservoir. Today Hentschel, at 48, is the founder and CEO of the third largest female-owned corporation in California.[7] She is the mother of seven, five who were adopted, and wife to resort owner Gordon Hentschel.

When Rev. Camille Russell, pastoral assistant at Faithful Central Mission Baptist Church in Inglewood, California, was asked how she interpreted her "women values" in her leadership role, she responded, "I love to lead by empowering people to do what they already do well, especially when they don't recognize it."

"After observing their personality, assessing their gifts, and hearing their passion, I encourage them into doing tasks that they usually do well. I then function as a facilitator of the talents and gifts," she said.

Rev. Russell compares herself to the captain of a ship. "I plot the course and point in the right direction. I make sure everyone knows that they are needed to get to our destination, but I don't do their job (at least I try not to). I let the cooks know that they need to feed the passengers. I make sure the custodians have everything they need to clean the ship. I assign people to their posts, and I go back to doing my specialty, steering the wheel and making sure we are on the right course." She sounds like a leader.[8]

Dr. Jacquelyn F. Jordan is associate professor of nursing at Western Connecticut State University. As a nurse, she served a three-year term in the United States Army during the Vietnam conflict. When asked about her guiding leadership principles, Dr. Jordan reflected "women values" in spite of military service. She responded, "Most decisions do not require an immediate response. Thus, I do not respond hastily without giving thought to it. At minimum, one must "sleep on it." Another principle to which she subscribes is "listen and reflect on what has been said. It is often what has not been said wherein the answer lies." She also believes saying "yes" to children is the path of least resistance. As parents, she said, "We must remember that 'tough love' yields more meaningful rewards."

The Honorable Carolyn J. B. Howard, of the 24th legislative district in the State of Maryland, expresses "women values" gleaned from experiences. She lists the value of leadership by example. The traditional leadership idea of "do as I say" gives way to "do as I do." Here, a person follows a leader not because they have to, but because they want to.

"Maintaining a professional demeanor and work environment is crucial," she says. "By providing a stable work environment, employees better function in their specific roles. It is especially important for those in supervisory positions to maintain a professional attitude because employees will follow the example set by those in charge."

In the women's leadership model, Aburdene and Naisbitt suggest that women leaders want people to speak up and act up. In the traditional male model of leadership, instead, the leader demands respect.

"Always speak up," says Howard. "Simply put, my opinion counts and is worthy to be heard. Being a public official, it is also essential that I listen to the concerns of my constituents and represent their interests."

Ellen Howard, whose most memorable role as an actress is the portrayal of the beautiful Carla Binary Hall on television's "One Life to Live" in the 1970s, believes that integrity and honesty are the core values that lie at the heart of all that she has done, personally and professionally. Her leadership is described as focusing on inspiring individual personalities. "Her style is to enable one to function as a single powerful unit greater than the sum of all it parts—to function, in other words, as a super team."

Women's experiences thus become the lenses through which those who are leaders view their role and function. They are the foundational groundwork from which our values rise and take shape, the places where our principles are first tested and tried.

Experiences shape us. They shape us like the rivers that carve out valleys and the wind and rain that shape mountains.

A PERSONAL JOURNEY

My fascination with leadership can be traced to my early childhood experiences. Leadership was never an option in my family. It was the rule rather than the exception. Leadership was something that was done on a regular basis like eating, breathing, or sleeping. What leadership looked like, smelled like, and acted like was an inherited expectation. It was as if it came with our genes and chromosome package like the color of our hair, eyes, and skin. It was the torch that was passed from one generation to the next. Sometimes it was passed whether you wanted it or not. Some family members came kicking and screaming to their leadership roles. Others took to it like a baby to a mother's breast.

My great-grandfather, John H. Murphy Sr., founded *The Afro-American* newspaper over one-hundred-and-nine years ago in 1892. In those waning years of the 1800s, he drank from the bitter cup of racism and poverty. He had ten children—five boys and five girls—to raise. It was a challenge, at best, on his whitewasher wages and his wife's butter-and-egg money.

He had started a Sunday school helper newspaper at Bethel A.M.E Church in Baltimore, Maryland. He served as the chair protem of the trustee board for sixteen years, as well as serving as Sunday school superintendent of the old Hagerstown District. He also sang and was president of the senior choir.

When the printing equipment of a failed publishing enterprise became available, Murphy purchased it with two hundred dollars of his wife's butter-and-egg money. He was going to publish a newspaper for the African Americans when only one-half of one percent of the community could read at the time.

Murphy started the business because he wanted a place where his children would always have a job and "where no white man would call me by my first name." *The Afro-American* newspaper grew to be one of the largest chains of black weekly newspapers. At one time, its editions included New England; Philadelphia; New Jersey; Richmond, Virginia; and the south. Today, The Afro-American Newspaper Company publishes *The Baltimore Afro-American* newspaper, *The Washington Afro-American* newspaper, *Every Wednesday,* and *The Afro Chronicles*.

It is amazing how experiences shape us. My first word after "mama" and "papa" was probably "deadline." I grew up surrounded by newspaper people: publishers, writers, editors, marketing and public relations people, circulation managers, and advertising experts. They were my baby-sitters and role models. My time after school was spent hanging around the office. I got into every department. I learned how to roll newspapers for mailing, work the addressing machine, set hot type, read backwards and upside down, lay out pages, and operate the switchboard.

It was at the *Baltimore Afro-American* newspaper or at my grandfather's house, Dr. Carl J. Murphy, then chairman of the board and publisher of The Afro-American Newspaper Company, where I observed the leaders of the world. I watched Dr. Martin Luther King Jr., Roy Wilkins, Jesse Jackson, Althea Gibson, Marion Anderson, Asa Phillip Randolph, Thurgood Marshall, Howard University's president Dr. Mordecai Johnson, Morgan State's president Dr. Martin Jenkins, and civil rights activists Clarence and Juanita Mitchell.

There were no formal leadership dialogues. There were no parental admonitions, required workshops, homework assignments, or leader seminars to attend. There were countless opportunities to observe some of the world's greatest leaders.

My grandfather was blessed with five daughters, one of them my mother, Ida Murphy Peters. The Murphy girls, who included a set of twins, became the "sons" he never had. All sixteen grandchildren carry the Murphy name.

Long before suffragettes, feminism, or women's liberation, there were the Murphy women taking on leadership roles. They ran whole newspaper departments, managed newspapers in other cities and states, became World War II correspondents, and were marketing and advertising pioneers and editors.

Great grandmother Martha Elizabeth Murphy was one of the organizers of the first "colored" YWCA's in Baltimore. Great Aunt Frances Murphy started the first urban environmental program, "The Clean Block Campaign," in Baltimore in the 1930s. Grandmother Vashti Turley Murphy was one of twenty-two founders of Delta Sigma Theta Sorority, Inc., in 1913. This is the largest public service organization in the world of college-trained

African American women numbering over two hundred thousand.

My mother and her sisters carried on the leadership legacy. My aunt Elizabeth Murphy Moss was the editor of *The Baltimore Afro-American* newspaper. Her column, "If You Asked Me," gave readers an opportunity "to read something good." Aunt Vashti Murphy Matthews was a World War II veteran, and her twin, Carlita Murphy Jones, was an educator in Buffalo, New York.

Aunt Frances Murphy II is the former chairman of the board of directors of The Afro-American Newspaper Company. She retired as publisher of *The Washington Afro-American* newspaper.

My mother was an advertising innovator, initiating popular cooking shows and bridal shows on college campuses. She organized merchants along the once infamous Pennsylvania Avenue, the heart of the black community. Her career spanned fifty-six years. She was known as Baltimore's "Clean Block Lady," or as "Mrs. Santa," raising thousands of dollars annually to beautify city neighborhoods and bring toys and food to hurting families during the Christmas holidays.

She became nationally known as the "entertainment editor" of *The Afro.* She developed the entertainment department in the late 1960s. She interviewed the greats and near-greats such as Bill Cosby, Harry Bellafonte, Sidney Poitier, Sammy Davis Jr., and Leontyne Price. She was invited to movie sets and major movie openings. Her columns and pages won national awards. I was just glad to go along for the ride!

The family's rite of passage was working at *The Afro.* We all did it sometime in our leader journey. I started writing a column for *The Afro* in high school called "All about You and Others" and, later, "The McKenzie Report." I worked on the city desk in the summer time, writing news stories and taking news tips from the telephone. I had no idea that I would go from writing obituaries to preaching them.

The leadership legacy continues. Cousin Rev. Frances Murphy Draper is the former president of The Afro-American Newspaper Company. Yvonne (Bonnie) Murphy Matthews publishes her own entertainment guide. Pat Lottier publishes *The Atlanta Tribune* in Atlanta, Georgia. Christopher Murphy Rabb publishes on the Internet. The rest of us content ourselves with careers in medicine, law, computer science, religion, the arts, business, as officers in the armed forces, and in corporate America.

There were countless, unspoken lessons on leadership taught by strong role models. I learned from each of them. Aunt Betty taught me how to network. Aunt Frankie taught me to go with your strength. Aunt Carlita taught me that you could work and raise a healthy family at the same time. Aunt Vashti taught me how to juggle more than one assignment at a time.

My grandmother taught me about the value of being an "iron fist in a velvet glove." Her strength was not loud and boisterous, its quiet tendrils would wrap around confusion and disruption rendering them null and void.

My mother taught me compassion. She was the pioneer and innovator who showed you that it was permissible to journey into new territories. She would say, "Your gifts were permission enough to exercise them. Be strong. We are not here to drift or dream. There are miles to go and loads to lift. Be strong."

These empowered leader women who moved effectively in career and community surrounded me. This is the ground of my leader beginnings. This is my women's experience, a rich reservoir that is a legacy, not a privilege. This is not true in every leader's life. My experience may be considered the exception rather than the rule. Or is it?

Patricia Reid-Merritt in *Sister Power* interviewed forty-five women of African descent who exerted great power and influence in various careers from the country's powerhub cities. Twelve were leaders in coporate America and the rest were leaders in the public area. She noted seven characteristics about the leader women. These are: has a strong family, had church and community support at an early age, are focused on identifiable goals, possess humanistic values, are spiritual, are political, are self-accepting as women, are grounded in their history, and are socially conscious.[9]

My early experiences had a profound effect upon my leadership journey. My family was a great source of strengh and motivation against the backdrop of a community that was less than positive about women in nontraditional roles. The seeds of leadership were planted and nourished in my youth. The fruit was harvested in my adult life. Time elapsed. Attitudes about women in nontraditional roles relaxed or became a matter of law. However, what was policy may not be true for praxis. What my family gave me bore fruit in my adult life in a community that was still less than positive about women in nontraditional roles.

The majority of the women responding to the survey indicated that family and early significant experiences played an important role in their leadership development.

Ellen Howard, a respondent to the "Strength in the Struggle" survey, feels that it is the combination of the early experiences with racism and sexism that creates a new leadership of vision that is able to survive all barriers.

Howard says that her mother, Grayce Arnold Howard, was her source of strength that modeled leadership. "She was a person capable of giving love to those she cared about unconditionally. Likewise, she invested herself one hundred percent in everything she did. Her life was a work of art," she writes.

Dr. Geraldine Pittman Woods wrote, "My mother did not have much formal training, but she had great wisdom. She shared that with me and told me to work harder and 'keep at it' until my task was accomplished. She told me to always be patient and appreciative of all things."

Dr. Woods graduated with a doctor of philosophy degree in neuro-embrology in 1945 from Radcliffe College and Harvard University. She later served as special consultant to the National Institutes of General Medical Sciences. The former national president of Delta Sigma Theta Sorority, Inc., she initiated and helped develop the Minority Access to Research Careers (MARC), later becoming the first woman to be elected chair of the board of trustees of Howard University.

Rev. Russell states that, along with God, her encouragement came from her family. "She [her mother] has always stood behind me and supported me physically, emotionally, and financially. One of the best things she did was allow me to be me. She allowed me to make my own mistakes and win my own victories. She takes the position as my number one cheerleader. A strong family support system helped as well. My grandmother and other extended family members were always there to support me."

Architect, planner, and program manger Cheryl L. McAfee's early family experiences were important to fulfilling her dreams. "They educated me; they taught me to read, comprehend, analyze, and write; they helped me to explore all of my gifts; they provided the many means for me to do and accomplish every dream I had."

Stephanie Rankin, executive director of a human services agency, reports, "If it had not been for the women in my family living leadership everyday, I would have given up a long time ago. You couldn't pick up a magazine, newspaper, or watch television without getting the impression that you did not have a future in the careers that were calling your name. My mother and sisters didn't buy the lie, and neither will I. Lead on!"

Osceola McCarty was denied a full education. She dropped out of school in the sixth grade to take care of an ailing aunt. When that aunt died, it was too late for her to go back to school. All she could do was to make a living doing what she knew how to do—wash clothes. She applied her learned lessons of hard work and thrift to her washerwoman business. McCarty worked from sunrise to sunset taking care of other people's clothes. In order to survive, she saved what she didn't need to spend.

Health forced her into retirement. She consulted with her banker, who handled her savings and investments. She decided to share the fruit of her labors with her family, church, and Mississippi State College.

This retired wash and iron woman gave $250,000 to an institution of higher learning. She never matriculated beyond grade school.

She'd never seen or attended the school. She wanted other children to have what she was denied—a college education. She did it all without owning a car or having a husband. Experiences shape us.

When Alex Haley was growing up, he heard the stories of his ancestors that had been recited throughout several generations. He traced these ancestral stories and preserved them in his seminal literary work, *Roots.*

As a little girl in her hometown of Eatonville, Florida, noted Harlem Renaissance writer Zora Neale Hurston listened to stories told at the general store. She later collected folktales and was admired for her gifts of story telling. Experiences shape us.

Jim and Jill Kelly wanted a son. When little Hunter was born, they were excited. The joy soon turned to pain when the baby was diagnosed with a rare disease. Hunter had no motor skill and his life expectancy was between thirteen months and two years.

Jim Hunter, one of the NFL superstars, started a foundation. Hunter's Hope was dedicated to educate the people about the disease and raise funds for research. Experiences shape us.

Jesse grew up in a household filled with fear and hostility. She watched her mother being physically assaulted by her father, and she was verbally abused by her father. She promised herself that if she survived her childhood, she would try to help others. She organized a hotline for families like hers. She is a counselor for abused women and children. Experiences shape us.

All the early events in our lives, from birth order, sibling rivalries, school experiences, environment, joys to sorrows, all impact our lives in various degrees. Later experiences serve to affirm or confirm the truth we have gleaned from them. On the other hand, events challenge us to use skills we didn't know we had or challenge us to draw from previously unexplored wells of strength.

Some of these events are positive and negative. We carry pieces of them around with us all our lives. Those pieces become close friends or troubling enemies. They are "the because of" and the "in spite of" our personalities. They are the guidance system of our behavior, the foundation upon which we place the personality building blocks of our existence, and the lens through which we view the world.

Experiences may not make or break a leader. They will provide the skeletal structure whereby the flesh of leader skills, styles, or behaviors will be added. Leadership in our family was more like a legacy than a privilege. It was never taken for granted or lightly. Each generation was expected to take the level of leadership higher. In such cases, the mantel of leadership could either lift you up or weigh you down. Its presence could inspire or overwhelm. In any case, this is the ground of my leadership beginnings. Experiences shape us.

One of actress Ellen Howard's guiding principles is "Learn how to enjoy the process of reaching a goal." It is just as important to learn as one attempts to reach goals, not just to reach them.

Our experiences are a part of the process we go through to reach goals. Another part of the process, defining moments, will be discussed in the next chapter.

Chapter three

Defining Moments

❦

E XPERIENCES SHAPE US. Within those ordinary, and often extraordinary, experiences of our lives are "Defining Moments." Defining moments are more than mere events or occa-
sions. These moments have the power to change our lives forever.
Life before defining moments and after defining moments is different. We think different. We feel different. We act different. We
respond and react differently.

Defining moments may be one or a series of experiences or events
that change the way we see things. Through its matrix of emotions,
feelings and challenges, both positive and negative, our view of life is
different. It is as if the lens of the glasses through which we view life
has been changed.

We were blinded by the bright light of tragedy and begin to
look back at life through darkened lens. Events took us far away
from our comfort zones and we do not know how to return.
Trouble hit too close to home and we do not want to leave its
security again.

After a defining moment it is difficult viewing the world again
in the same manner. An unexpected pregnancy, a spouse dies, children leave the nest, retirement, employment is terminated, or ter-
minal illnesses are moments that can cause a shift in outlook as
new realities emerge. A promotion or a raise may change the rules
of a relationship on the job and in the home.

Our perceptions are changed by the defining moment. Just as
indelible ink stains the writing surface permanently, these moments
stain the papyrus of our lives. Defining moments create the critical
mass from which new habits are born. They are the triggers that
alter our behavior patterns.

Priorities change because this climacteric pause in our lives force us to examine what really is important. Things that mattered prior to the "defining moment" are challenged in the vortex of the experience. If when weighed in the balance of the event, they still have merit, the priorities continue. If not, they lose their potency. The priority is cast aside like a favorite sweater that no long fits, shoes that are too small, or an activity you've outgrown. When I was a child, I spoke like a child, I thought like a child, I reasoned like a child; when I became an adult, I put an end to childish ways (1 Cor. 13:11).

David's defining moment was Goliath. His childhood experiences prepared him for the confrontation near the valley of Elah (1 Sam. 17). He learned valuable lessons keeping daddy's sheep. It was in solitude that the young shepherd drew close to God. It was on a lonely hillside he first began to sing psalms. It was in protecting the sheep from the lion and bear that David found his strength. These were the experiences that laid the foundation for the future.

Jesse's youngest son was tried on the grazing fields before he met an enemy no one else wanted to tackle. The soldier saw Goliath as a muscle mass of gigantic proportions: nine-feet-tall, carrying a spear the size of a weaver's beam with an iron point weighing six hundred shekels or fifteen pounds.

All David saw was an uncircumcised Philistine who had the nerve to defy the armies of God. It was a problem to King Saul and his army. It was an opportunity for David to champion his God.

David was an unlikely leader. He did not have military experience. He was not schooled in military strategy. He did not know how to handle a soldier's armor. He was old enough to be sent to inquire about his brothers.

David responded to the threat of sword, javelin, and spear by using familiar weapons. He used a slingshot and a stone. He used a spiritual weapon, the name of the Lord of Hosts, the God of the armies of Israel (1 Sam. 17:45).

The unlikely leader defeated the enemy. David was no longer the shepherd boy and harp player. He was transferred from the choir to a high rank in the army. He was now a courageous military strategist who successfully defeated God's enemies. Things changed forever after that day in the Valley of Elah. This was David's defining moment.

Eve and Adam's defining moment was an incident in the garden about a tree and an apple. Adam received instructions for paradise maintenance from God. The rule was made perfectly clear. They had access to every part of paradise except one tree, the tree of good and evil.

That sounded simple enough. As soon as you are told not to do something, you immediately want to do it. Make a decision to go on a diet and even food you don't usually eat will find its way into your mouth. Tell a child they can't go somewhere special that day and they will want to go all the more. You are told that you can't have something and you'll want it all the more.

Eve was lured by the deception of the serpent in the garden. Eve ate first and gave it to Adam. Although both were guilty, Eve's gender has borne the burden of the disobedience. It took the resurrection of Jesus the Christ to handle the consequence from this defining moment.

Esther's defining moment was the crisis that precipitated her going to see the king uninvited and unannounced. Haman's plot to eradicate the Jews was set in motion; the king signed the order for their annihilation. Mordecai, Esther's uncle and mentor, approached her to intercede.

Within the context of her position as queen, Esther demonstrated leadership in organizing her household and cleverly approaching the problem of genocide. She facilitated a solution at great risk to her own life.

Defining moments can be specific and personal, such as a divorce or the death of a spouse, parent, or child. They can be ordinary things that most people experience, such as getting your first job, going on your first date, healing from your first broken heart, having your first baby. They can be ordinary experiences with extraordinary results.

Defining moments can be catastrophic, such as experiencing life-threatening situations: an earthquake, hurricane, tornado, or being swept away in a flood. They can be accidents that threaten body, mind, and spirit.

Defining moments can be communal or societal. These formidable moments impact not only the individual, but also groups of people within a society. It effects a segment or the entire population for generations to come.

What were your societal defining moments? It could be the United States Senate hearings on Justice Clarence Thomas's appointment to the Supreme Court. Prof. Anita Hill had charges of sexual harassment that the committee was refusing to hear. Women rose up to demand that Hill be heard. The testimony she gave ricocheted across the country. It changed workplace etiquette for both men and women. It spurned new employment policies.

Is your societal defining moment the O.J. Simpson trial? The trial brought the issue of spousal abuse to the front pages of newspapers around the world. The trial in the court of public opinion and in the court of law lowered the tolerance level of rich bad boys. The public defrocking of an American hero was traumatic for some. It also raised new questions about an African American male receiving a fair trial in the American justice system.

The Great Depression was a defining moment for millions who lost jobs, homes, and families during the economic disaster. World War II, the Korean War, and the Vietnam War were defining moments for men and women who fought, the families who waited, and the families for whom soldiers did not come home.

The assassinations of John F. Kennedy, Robert Kennedy, Martin Luther King Jr., and Medgar Evers was a defining moment for many living in the turbulent times of the 1960s. The assassination of Tupac Sukur and Biggie Smalls were defining moments for Generation X. While baby boomers lit candles, cried, and held vigils for the leaders ripped from our society, the hip-hop generation did the same for their fallen heroes.

The Watergate scandal, Monica Lewinsky, the bull Wall Street market, Sammy Sousa, and Mark McGuire breaking Babe Ruth's record, or the Baltimore Ravens winning the 2001 Super Bowl are defining moments. Life will never be the same again.

Japanese internment camps were defining moments for thousands of Japanese Americans during World War II. Jews annihilated in German concentration camps; Haitians denied political asylum; Cubans traveling the ninety miles to Miami, Florida, the best way they could; and Africans stolen from their homeland—these are defining moments. The basic societal defining moments that have had the greatest impact upon the lives of women, generally, and women of African descent, particularly, are enslavement, consistent racism, and sexism.[1]

We have never gotten over enslavement. When we self-destruct, is this post-traumatic stress syndrome? The trauma of enslavement has sown seeds that continue to be harvested a century later. It doesn't matter whether you were born close to the holocaust of slavery or decades later. Africans came first to America as explorers, artisans, and hired servants. Later, they were taken against their will and brought to this country as free labor to fuel the emerging economy of the colonies.

Images of both men and women of African descent rose to justify their maltreatment. African women were portrayed as either "Mammy" or "Jezebel." To many, she was just a breeder, mother, cook, or housekeeper, less than human, whose mission was to serve. She may have been in charge of the kitchen and the nursery, but she was not in charge of her life.

The Jezebel image characterized African women as evil—loose, carnal vixens who shamelessly tempted men into sexual activities. This image along with Mammy emerge in later generations as Carmen Jones of "Sweet Georgia Brown" fame and Aunt Jemima of pancake fame.

Today's generation of gangsta rap productions has been accused of reinventing the image of Jezebel. They seem to reduce women in their songs to mere body parts. Women are seen as devoid of personality and character and are a mere assemblage of body parts—hips, lips, and mammary glands.

Enslavement was a defining moment for women of African descent. Everything changed—their environment, culture, society, socioeconomic order, language, country, and position. They went from copartners in family and community-building to nonhuman entity. Enslaved men of African descent were counted by the United States as three-fifths of a man. Women were not counted at all.

Enslavement for women was different than for men. Women suffered the additional atrocities of rape, perversion, and sexual exploitation. Enslavement has sown seeds of mistrust, fear, anger, low self-esteem, and self-hate. The seeds continue to bear fruit in later generations, triggered by the defining moments of consistent racism and sexism.

Consistent racism is like an invisible film coating everything. You can see where you want to go but it is like fighting your way through Saran Wrap to get there. The invisible film deftly separates one ethnic group from another, even in this post-Civil Rights era. Publicly, racism invisibly dips below the radar scanner until it glaringly erupts from police brutality to job discrimination. Privately, it acts as an invisible shield, protecting one ethnic group from another. "I have been raised with the expectation of racism. Because of this expectation I have learned how to cope. Learning of those who have gone before me to fight the monster of racism makes me proud to be of a people of strength," states Rev. Camille Russell of Los Angeles, California.

Actress Ellen Howard indicates that she has faced both racism and sexism. She believes that what she set out to do in life remains undone. Howard has persisted in overcoming any timidity to tackle her goals because of these obstacles.

Sexism is a defining moment. It creates an additional burden for all women. Gender can disqualify you from the leadership arena in spite of your qualifications, training, education, gifts, skills, and talents. It is like striking out before you get a chance to swing at the ball. A home run is needed, but there are people who are afraid that the woman just may hit it over the fence.

Cheryl L. McAfee, president of Charles F. McAfee Architects and Planners in Atlanta, Georgia, said that she first had to come to the realization that racism and sexism belongs to racists and the sexists. She ponders about how does the victim of rape overcome:

I use this analogy to suggest victims of sexism and racism are raped of self esteem, are violated and discouraged; are humiliated and become paranoid. To overcome, I realize that someone else is very sick and thay someone else is wrong about his or her interpretation of my person. I know in whose image I was created and to whom I belong. God moves that which would be an impediment and makes it a stepping-stone. Instead of being a victim, I become the victor.[2]

She went on to say that, "No matter what the challenge is, I go through it with the assurance that God is with me and that I will endure any and every challenge this life may bring."

"To those who would be racist, or sexist, or just evil," said McAfee, "I pray for them and their problem and that the Lord might bring about a change in their life that might lead them to a better understanding of God and God's love for them."

"Sexism is new to me," says Rev. Russell. "Confrontation in the area of sexism manifests itself whenever I assert myself as a woman called and anointed by God. Questions arise, attitudes persist, comments are made, all in all in an attempt to keep me from walking in my authority." As red is a deeper shade of pink, defining moments are a deeper shade of experiences. Defining moments can change our hopes dreams and fears. They affect our relationships. Our parenting, job performance, psyches, emotions, social consciousness, self-esteem, values, and self-worth are affected by defining moments. Leadership, too.

GLEANING LEADER LESSONS

A young girl by the name of Dorothy lived in a gray house in the middle of a gray prairie where nothing was seen between her house and the horizon. There was not a tree, hill, barn, or house. It was all flat ground as far as the eye could see. She came to Aunt Em and Uncle Henry's house as an orphan. Her laughter brightened their gray Kansas world.

Dorothy had a defining moment. It changed her life forever. She went from playing with a little dog to finding her way home and leading three men to their heart's desire. There are leader lessons to be learned in this classic children's story. Here is Dorothy on leadership—"Toto, we're not in Kansas anymore."

There are several pieces of literature that have the distinction of transcending the written page and are reinterpreted in other media as well. An example is Alice Walker's *The Color Purple*, or Alex Haley's *Roots*, and Louisa Mae Alcott's *Little Women*. These are venerable favorites to more than one generation. L. Frank Baum's children's classic, *The Wonderful Wizard of Oz*, is another.

Written in 1900, Baum stated in the introduction that the book aspired to be "a modernized fairy tale, in which the wonderment and joy are retained and the heartaches and nightmares are left out."

It started out as stories told in the evening by Baum to his children. One hundred years later, Dorothy, the Scarecrow, Lion, and Tin Man are cultural icons with an international fan club. The yellow brick road, Munchkins, Winged Monkeys, Winkies, and the Emerald City have all worked their way into our vocabulary. Judy Garland immortalized "Somewhere Over the Rainbow" in the movie version.

The Wonderful Wizard of Oz has been loved and enjoyed by multitudes. It's colossal success on television and the silver screen has consistently brought this tale to life time after time. It's characters are known worldwide. There have been plays, artwork, toys, and more. It has been politicized and psychoanalyzed. Teachers even use *Oz* lesson plans in the classroom. This is a story about a little girl named Dorothy who was "sunshine on a cloudy day" in the gray Kansas world of Aunt Em and Uncle Henry. Hard prairie living had changed a young, pretty wife into a gaunt woman who never smiled. Uncle Henry never smiled, but worked the land the best he could. Toto's playful nature kept Dorothy from becoming a part of the gray world.

Everyone was working except Dorothy. She just played with Toto.

In the movie, Dorothy is shown exploring her Kansas world. Was it boredom? Was it curiosity that sent her from home that fateful day? Was it simply too much play?

In any case, Dorothy was not paying attention. She was neither aware nor conscious of her surroundings. Maybe this was her first cyclone season and she didn't know the peril and power of this kind of a storm. She may not have had enough sense to watch out for the warning signs: gathering storm clouds, increase in the wind, stationary objects moving, or calls to safety.

Dorothy Leadership Lesson Number One: Be aware of what is happening in your environment. Leaders must be vigilant. They must be aware of activity and action going on around them. Wake up and read the weather report. Discern the warning signs: disgruntled coworkers, personnel coming in late all the time, increase in sick leave, unauthorized purchases, unreturned phone calls, or missed deadlines.

An inattentive leader will be caught off guard if trouble should come. Learn how to read the weather forecast in your work environment. Look for the warning signs of rain because when it rains, it pours. It is important to know when a cold shoulder front is moving in. A high-pressure assignment may be on the way requiring overtime over the weekend. A flood of resignations may occur because of the rainstorm. A hurricane may force you to move to the higher ground of upper management for relief. Read the warning signs or, before you know it, you may be caught up in a whirlwind.

That's exactly what happened to Dorothy. Before she realized it, she was caught up in a whirlwind. Aunt Em and Uncle Henry made it to the storm cellar, but Dorothy was caught by the storm trying to retrieve Toto.

Dorothy Leadership Lesson Number Two: Never get so far away that you cannot get back to safety in time. We have all known women who were not paying attention to their lives and got caught up in a whirlwind. Before they realized it, they were fired, burned-out, pregnant, addicted, overdrawn, or were too far away to get to safety in time because of a dog.

The whirlwind cyclone lifted the house from the ground. It

was caught in the vortex, tossing its contents around. When the house landed, Dorothy was deposited in a place that she did not recognize. Baum wrote in the original introduction that every healthy youngster loved stories that were "fantastic, marvelous, and manifestly unreal."

Dorothy's defining moment was an unreal situation. Everything was different in the Land of Oz. There was a different cast of characters and a different culture from Kansas's prairie life. There was a different language, rules, and policies.

Aunt Em and Uncle Henry, her mentors, were no longer there to protect her. Her home was destroyed and she was without credit card, cell phone, or fax machine. There was a new power structure in place that did not include her. All she had was Toto.

Dorothy committed an irreversible act. She killed the Wicked Witch of the East. The witch's sister, the Wicked Witch of the West, would want to take revenge. This all could end up very nasty and could cost Dorothy more than she was willing to give. Toto, we're not in Kansas anymore!

Dorothy Leadership Lesson Number Three: Be careful where you land. There are times when we get caught in a whirlwind. It may be a mess of our own making or you may be an innocent bystander.

When the wind dies down and things settle down watch where you land. When things are out of control, everyone hopes for a soft landing: reassigned to a new area; transferred to another department, another city, or another country; a slap on the wrist; or a memo in the personnel file. Hard landings are hard for everyone: discrimination suit, bankruptcy, plant-closing, firing a friend, or being fired. Trying to maintain equilibrium in a cyclone of a situation is hard. Do not bring anyone down with you. Do not; I repeat, do not kill anyone.

Dorothy had lots of excuses to offer. It was not me but the house that killed her. It was the whirlwind that started it all. It was Aunt Em's fault for not warning me in time.

Dorothy learns in Munchkin Land there is no shedding of tears or gnashing of teeth over the loss of the Wicked Witch of the East.

In fact, the Munchkins are grateful to her for taking this ugly problem off their hands. Blessed Dorothy! What could have been a horrible mess leading to charges of manslaughter has been averted.

Dorothy Leadership Lesson Number Four: Try to make the best out of every bad situation. The cash flow is low; tighten the belt and prioritize. Several employees are on leave; bring in temps. (Temporary help or use college interns.) Stock is gone; hold a press conference and announce your sales success. Witch dead; get the ruby red slippers!

Dorothy wants to go home but does not know the way. It is hard to get back to where you started from if you don't know where you are. No one has heard of Kansas, but they are willing to point her in the direction of the Emerald City. There is a wizard there who knows everything. The Wizard of Oz can help Dorothy get home. All she has to do is follow the Yellow Brick Road and keep a grip on the ruby red slippers.

Dorothy Leadership Lesson Number Five: Know where you stand. Pay attention as you go along in life just in case you have to go back by yourself. Take notes. Keep a journal. Ask questions. Do research and analyze the data. Keep track of your gains and loses. Obtain reports. Do reports. Keep reports on file. Get a map. Get satellite tracking in the car. Leave a trail of crumbs if you have to, but know where you stand.

Dorothy is trying to leave when she has just arrived. Along the Yellow Brick Road she encounters three characters, the Scarecrow, the Lion, and the Tin Man. Each of them has problems. Who doesn't? Dorothy suggests that they go with her to see the wizard in Emerald City.

She is developing into quite a little leader. Remember, a leader is one who gains a consensus and leads others towards a specific goal. You go girl! Dorothy is taking advantage of collective action. She is still on the hit list of the Wicked Witch of the West. She is a female minor traveling in unfamiliar territory among unknown dangers. These traveling companions could mentor her through this crisis. They could interpret her surroundings: poppy fields, witches brooms, Winkies, and Winged Monkeys. They could also provide protection.

The only problem is she sought help from those who couldn't help themselves. She solicited the help of a man with no brain, a lion with no courage, a man with no heart, and a wizard with no power. Yet, they skipped together to find what was missing in their lives down the Yellow Brick Road.

Dorothy Leadership Lesson Number Six: Work with what you've got. We would all like to work in perfect places with perfect bosses, perfect coworkers, perfect resources, perfect salaries, perfect attitudes, perfect tools, and perfect agendas. Life should be so sweet!

Learn to work with what you have until something better comes along. It may mean additional in-house training, conference attendance, college courses, and follow-up meetings. It may necessitate adjusting to the particular needs of your coworkers. Keep lots of oil on hand for all the tin men. Keep extra straw in stock for the scarecrows, and no fair picking on the lions. It takes some people a little longer to get the hang of things. Work with them. They may not look like much, but they can get you to the Emerald City

Dorothy was able to make friends with all the men in her life: Uncle Henry, the Scarecrow, the Tin Man, the Lion and, eventually, the Wizard. Working with the women was another story.

There was not one sister-girlfriend in Dorothy's life. She is cavorting 'round a strange countryside with three adult male personalities. There is no one of her age in her life in Oz or Kansas. She is having problems with the adult women in her life. She didn't listen to Aunt Em and ended up in a whirlwind. She killed one woman. Another woman is out to kill her. Glenda, the Good Witch is so busy that she is in and out of Dorothy's life. Dorothy was able to be friends with all the men but not the women. She worked well with the men but not with all the women.

Dorothy Leadership Lesson Number Seven: Develop relationships with both men and women. There are women who have the Dorothy Syndrome. They relate to men better than women, are more comfortable around men, prefer working with men.

It has nothing to do with sexual orientation. They just take and receive instructions easier from men than from women. They'd rather contend with a man than a woman for a title, position, or the boss's favor. They have more in common with what the men are doing rather than what the women are about.

Dorothy and her three coworkers reached the Emerald City. The trip was not without incident. The forest was scary. The Scarecrow lost some straw and the Tin Man got wet and rusted. They arrived without notice or an appointment. When they tried to access power, they were denied. The three finally negotiated a deal. The great Wizard of Oz would grant Dorothy's request if she rendered her services. She had to bring back the broom of the Wicked Witch of the West to him. After all, she obtained the ruby red slippers from the Wicked Witch of the East, why not get her sister's broom?

Dorothy and the three companions went to the witch's castle. They had to travel through the forest of the Winged Monkeys. The Scarecrow, Tin Man, and Lion were no match for the flying creatures. They took Dorothy away from them and took her to the castle of the witch who wanted to kill her.

Was Dorothy so naive to think that the witch would just give it to her? She began conflict resolution procedures to negotiate terms to receive the broom. Things went from bad to worse. Toto's life was in jeopardy. Her three companions were attempting a felony—breaking and entering to reach her. In the end, Dorothy had to commit murder one more time. She melted the witch with water, took the broom, and returned to the Emerald City.

Dorothy Leadership Lesson Number Eight: Try to turn an enemy into a friend. Dorothy was no prize herself. She was guilty of manslaughter, thief of ruby red slippers, poppy-field running, and hanging around men not her age. She killed the woman's sister and was now coming to steal her broom.

There are sins on both sides of every argument. Look for ways to settle your differences. Attack the problem, not the personality. Disagree without being disagreeable. Get the facts. Compromise or collaborate if you have the time. Identify common interests. Don't trust your memory—get it in writing. If all else fails, throw water!

Dorothy did what was required of her. She risked her life and the lives of others to fulfill the assignment. She came back with the broom. All hail! The wicked witch is dead. The Winged Monkeys are now free. The inhabitants of the city rejoice that for a second time, a bad thing did some good.

She had limited experience in such things. She was working with a new staff. They had not previously worked together on an assignment. They exhibited team spirit. They had the courage of their conviction and confidence in themselves in spite of their individual problems. All of them were expecting the wizard to make good on his promise. They did their part, now it was management's turn to give out the rewards. One wanted a mind, the other a heart, another courage and, lastly, Dorothy to go back to the home office.

The Wizard had no power. They believed that he had the authorization to solve their problems. He did not. Consequently, he was exposed for who he really was—a man in wizard's clothing. The false wizard could, however, help the Scarecrow. He had already demonstrated intelligence. All he needed was affirmation. He received it. The Wizard helped the Lion who already displayed courage under fire. All he needed was commendation. He received it. The Wizard helped the Tin Man who already showed great compassion. All he needed was validation. He received it.

The Wizard tried to get Dorothy home himself. He succeeded in taking his own "golden" balloon out of the Emerald City, leaving Dorothy behind. That is what false wizards do. They help themselves and leave you behind.

Dorothy Leadership Lesson Number Nine: Be wary of false wizards. They are those persons who promise a lot and deliver little. They will promise you the world and give you a zip code. Watch out for those who are willing to risk your career and never put theirs on the line. They are willing to put your company, stock, and marriage in peril. All while sitting in their Emerald towers while watching you run search-and-seize missions.

It seems that no matter what you do, they will not be satisfied. After you have done the impossible, they jack-up the price. The hurdles will be higher and the race longer. What is done in secret will come to light. Burst their balloon and move on.

Dorothy ends the defining moment where she began, a long way from the home office. The only problem that remains is getting back to Kansas, Aunt Em, and Uncle Henry. Glenda, the Good Witch, returns to tell Dorothy that she was in possession of the solution to her problem all along. The ruby red slippers could take her home at any time. Click your heels three times and go home.

Dorothy Leadership Lesson Number Ten: Know your own power. Dorothy was unaware that she had the power to accomplish her task. She had gone through an arduous ordeal only to learn it was within reach all along.

It was not a loss. She met new people who demonstrated kindness and concern. She learned more about herself. Her courage was tested. Her skills were tried. She was thrust into a difficult situation and survived. Was it worth it?

Next time, check your weapons carefully. Make sure you have enough firepower and ammunition for the battles up the Yellow Brick Roads. Learn how to use your weapons so that you apply the proper response to the challenges you face.

Dorothy, the next time you find yourself in the Land of Oz, know the power you possess and the power available through Jesus Christ. "I can do all things through Jesus Christ."

Chapter four

Surviving the Jungle

༚

THE WORLD OF WORK in the twenty-first century, according to one expert, is best described as a jungle. Phil Porter speaks of the workplace as a jungle where you eat or are eaten alive.[1] He describes it as a savage jungle where bosses grab the lion's share of credit and subordinates flee the blame and responsibilities like frightened gazelles; back-stabbing colleagues lurk behind every tree. Prize assignments are often snares or traps in disguise. Only the cunning and resourceful make it to the top of the heap. It is a jungle out there!

Porter explains working environments as places where you grind or are grounded.[2] You cook or you'll be the main entree for lunch. The quicker, savvier, and ruthless predators are more likely to succeed. It is a jungle out there!

Leaders are to lead and survive in places where one employee is pitted against others. Each day resembles a fierce, no-holds-barred, WWF "Smack Down." There is brutal and savage combat just to get the report done, respond to management, and manage co-workers and family members, or just getting through the day. It is a jungle out there!

In this jungle, only the strong survive. The weak end up on the bottom of the food chain. The road to success is paved with the broken bodies of competitors. It takes more than know-how to do your job and do it well. A leader must also learn the survival skills and strategies. There are those who contend that you must also know the dirty tricks, underhanded methodologies, sneaky tactics, and below-the-belt punches that would make you pray to be "touched by an angel."

The jungle world of work clashes with the Realm of God. The jungle can be hazardous to your health. It can harm you. Jesus announced that the realm was at hand and something that was yet to come. He also presented the realm as a present reality manifested in his own ministry and person (Matt. 12:28). Thus the realm transformed the worst into the best. (Matt. 11:2).

The jungle is pompous, arrogant, and proud. The realm is humility (Matt. 5:10). The jungle is looking for the easy way out. It is about getting over rather than going through. The realm is going through hardship to enter into the realm of God (Luke 9:62).

In the jungle, you can talk a good game. The realm is more than talk, but power (1 Cor. 4:20). The jungle is survival of the fittest. The realm is the salvation of the whosoever (John 3:16). The jungle is littered with pink slips and bad news. There is the preaching of the Good News to the captives. He or she who dies with the most toys wins in the jungle. In the realm, he or she who believes in Jesus shall never die (John 11:25).

In the jungle it's, "You only go round once in life, grab all the gusto you can," or "It's me first and everyone else later." In the realm, you strive first for God's realm and his righteousness and then all these things will be given to you as well (Matt. 6:33). In the jungle, the wages of sin is death, but in the realm, the gift of God is eternal life (Rom. 6:23). In the jungle you can lie, cheat, and steal your way in. No one can enter into the realm of God unless they are born of water and the Spirit. Flesh gives birth to flesh. Spirit gives birth to spirit. (John 3:3–6) In the jungle you can be ravaged by competition, but Jesus has rescued you from the dominion of darkness and brought you into the marvelous light.

The jungle warfare of the world of work doesn't get along with the realm of God. It is like trying to mix oil and water. Shake it hard and long but it will not mix. In the end, the two substances will separate, the oil at the bottom and the water at the top. These two entities are contrary to the structural integrity of each other. They do exist parallel in the same world. Many times, realm-men and -women are caught between the two as living between a rock and a hard place.

How do we survive the jungle? The next series of sermons focus upon the leadership of Nehemiah, the cupbearer of the King. The first sermon, "Kick But" offers suggestions about handling opposition. "The Right Stuff" is the second, and this one is about learning to handle success and succession. The third, "It's a Love Thing, You Ought to Understand," wrestles with long-term problems.

THE WORD

> But when Sanballat the Horonite and Tobiah the Ammonite official, and Gesham the Arab heard of it, they mocked and ridiculed us saying, 'What is this you are doing?' Are you rebelling against the king?" Then I replied to them, 'The God of heaven is the one who will give us success, and we his servants are going to start building; but you have no share or claim or historic right in Jerusalem.—Nehemiah 2:19–20

Kick But

There are times in the history of our lives when God, in his providence, does the very thing we least expect. Times we are certain that our options are clear. Times when we are assured about the alternatives laid before us, only to find out that God is moving in an entirely different direction, one you'd least expect.

There are times you think God is functioning over here, only to find God moving over there. Times you thought that "the die is cast," and God inexplicably renders the impossible possible. Times when God was expected to be silent, Yet God spoke. Times when God was expected to act, only God deferred.

There were times when you knew God was angry and the Lord slipped into your bedroom late at night to tell you that he's slow to burn. Times when you knew judgment was coming, but grace showed up.

No one expected God to retrieve Moses from the wilderness. God did. No one expected God to speak from a burning bush.

God did. No one expected Aaron's rod to blossom or the Nile to turn to blood. It did.

No one expected God to withhold judgment from Nineveh after Jonah told them the prophecy of its coming. Tell me, who expected his son to be born through a humble, homeless couple far from the accouterments of royalty? No one expected a thief to ride in the front seat of the Lord's limousine into paradise. He did.

Jesus told them, but who really expected that cross on Calvary? No one expected the earth to shake and the sun to refuse to shine. No one expected that after the humiliation on Friday, there would be exaltation on Sunday.

There are times in the history of our lives when God, in his providence, does the very thing we would least expect. Our rational minds are unable to grasp it. Our reason is confused by it. The wise are confounded by its simplicity.

Predictability has long since given up on God. All predictability can say is that God's ways are not our ways. Perhaps, upon occasion, predictability is to be inscrutable, that is "past finding out." It is God going beyond our ability to grasp the fullness of it.

In the second chapter of Nehemiah, it may have been expected that God would leave well enough alone. God didn't. There had already been another attempt to rebuild the wall of Jerusalem under Ezra. Someone else had tried. They failed to rebuild the place where their fathers prayed and their bodies were buried.

It failed for a number of reasons. There was great opposition. The enemy gained an upper hand through jungle ambush sabotage strategies. The efforts of the Jews were undermined. The task was perhaps too large for the people to handle. It may have been expected that God would leave well enough alone. God didn't.

God also unexpectedly commissioned Nehemiah to do the rebuilding. He was a cupbearer to the Babylonian king, Artaxerxes, during the Second Captivity. He was a government worker who held a plush palace position within the enemy's camp.

Nehemiah was not a builder. He didn't have an engineering degree or experience running a construction site. He knew nothing of subcontractors and building materials. There is no indicated intimate knowledge of brick and mortar.

Nehemiah was a political appointee in the King's court; he had no leadership training or experience. He was not in charge of a great army. He simply risked his life to taste the king's food and wine first. It was a dangerous job, but someone had to do it. God did the unexpected again. God put Nehemiah in the driver's seat of the rebuilding program in Jerusalem.

God saw in Nehemiah what he hadn't seen in himself. It may have been revealed during the four months of prayer prior to embarking upon this venture (Neh. 2:1). It may have been fostered in a continued relationship with God, even while in exile. Leadership may have been born out of a heart of compassion for both people and place (Neh. 1:4).

Just because you cannot see what God sees in you, doesn't mean that it doesn't exist. God knew that Nehemiah could safely navigate a career change. He could go from cupbearer to building. There were skills in his former position that could be transferred to the new one. In order to be the king's cupbearer, Nehemiah had to be man who could be trusted. A man who could be in the same room where policies and politics are discussed. He would be a man who listened to the decisions and wisdom as they were rendered in the court of the king. The man was comfortable with his tasting tasks. He also interfaced with the heads of state as they visited the Babylonian king. The king could lean on him if necessary.

There are attributes in most positions that can be transferred. These include such things as honesty, integrity, morality, creativity, responsibility, imagination, follow-through, and courage. It does not matter what position you hold, ditchdigger, choir director, porter, doctor, lawyer, or Indian chief. These qualities are needed.

There is a tendency among some to only glory in visible prominent positions. Everyone cannot be the pastor, governor, councilperson, senator, mayor, chairperson, or chief executive officer. All leadership needs followership or back-up.

Nehemiah provided back-up for the king as a prelude to his own leadership assignment. Every leader needs back-up. Moses had Joshua. Saul had David. David had Jonathan. Ruth had Naomi. Jesus had John. Martha had the Vandellas. Smokey had the Miracles. Patti Labelle had the Bluebelles. Nehemiah may not have had direct training for the leadership position ahead, but he had the potential to learn.

The text indicates that Nehemiah approach his new position methodically. He waited for the right time to broach the subject with the king. He secured authority to go to Jerusalem to work on the walls. He left Babylon with soldiers to protect him and a requisition order for resources to begin the work.

He moved quietly around the city gathering information. He inspected the ruins. He assessed the job. The debris was so bad that he could not ride but had to dismount his donkey and walk. Nehemiah moved without a press conference or an entourage. He did not tell the priests, nobles, officials, or anyone what he was doing and who would do the work.

This was his season to incubate. This was his time to do a statistical analysis. This was his time to develop his vision statement including mission and goals. Nehemiah held his plan close to the chest as if he were afraid to tell it too soon.

Leaders must be careful not to tell too soon. Joseph had a God-given dream. The dream indicated his elevation but he told the dream to his brothers. Jealousy arose to delay the dream but not deny it.

In the fullness of time, Nehemiah shared with the other leaders: "You see the trouble we are in, how Jerusalem lies in ruins with its gates burned. Come, let us rebuild the wall of Jerusalem, so that we may no longer suffer disgrace" (Neh. 2:17).

He shared the vision. It was now no longer just Nehemiah's and God's idea. Now, the people could buy into the plan. It was not given as a task to yoke them but as a cause to inspire them. He indicated that this new, perhaps, unexpected venture was with divine direction. The hand of God was upon him. And, oh by the way, the king was also backing the project.

The people strengthened their hands and began the work. This is where the "but" shows up. Verses 19 and 20 of Nehemiah indicate dissension in the ranks. Three people, Sanballant, Tobiah, and Geshem heard about the new effort. Their minority report included a slur that this is not really renovation but a disguised rebellion against the king. This is a good jungle tactic—slander, criticism, and a hint that it may be the genesis of war. It had worked so well with Ezra, why not try the same tactic again.

Leadership had gained a consensus. The people were challenged and motivated. A plan of action was in place. The people were ready to work. Things were going so well. Then somebody raises a "but." How does this occasion in the life of Nehemiah the cupbearer, now Nehemiah the builder, help us face the "buts" when they come along in our life?

The first thing to keep in mind is to be careful of the company you keep. There are critical people who will wear you out and wear you down, emotionally and spiritually. Pull your life together and someone will show up to pull it apart. God tells you to move forward and there is always someone who shows up with the "but" list of reasons why it cannot be God.

"But," this is not a rebuilding project. This is rebellion. That's like saying you're not losing on a low salt, low sodium diet for healthy weight loss, you are trying to embarrass me. You're going back to school because I didn't finish. Your new make over was done to make me feel bad. Life is too short to waste worrying about critical personalities. Respond like Nehemiah, this is not about you. It's about God. God will grant us success.

Secondly, learn to evaluate the enemy. The enemy launched a critical attack, not a physical attack. It was an encounter with word, not weapons. The words were a carefully placed disapproval designed to dismantle the rising motivation and excitement. They didn't attack the job. They attacked the motivation. Nehemiah had all his ducks in order. The vision, mission, and goals were all in place. A survey was done to back up the rebuilding effort. A letter from the king provided support from the palace.

When Sanballat, Tobiah, and Geshem jumped out of the jungle, all they could do is throw mud on the purpose of the project. If the three could have stopped Nehemiah, they would have. All they could do was talk. That is known as selling wolf tickets. When the naysayers arrive, they do not have to stay. Do not allow the "buts" to wear you down.

Third, listen to God and not the opposition. The opposition will always have a negative tale to tell. It is their job. It is a part of their job description. Negative criticism is listed on the resume of opposition. They just can't help themselves.

Listen to what they have to say to see if there is any truth in their statement. Remember who is saying it and where they come from. When the criticisms are false, you move forward. There is always someone in the corner with a "but". Listen to God and not the opposition. God's word will teach you how to kick "but" in the jungle world of work, in the trenches of congregational life, or the minutia of community life.

The text says "but" there were three opposing the project. Nehemiah replied that the God he served has a response to your "but". He will prosper us, give us success, so let's rise up and build instead of losing sleep over the opposition. You cannot please every "but" in the house. Instead of biting nails, losing hair, going crazy, listen to what God says, not the op Dr. Johnny Youngblood told me once, "If God is in charge of the church, go to sleep!" God is the original "but" kicker in the jungle. God knows how to kick. Someone says, "But," you respond, "No weapon formed against me shall prosper." Another says, "But," and you respond, "Ye shall not need to fight in the battle. Set yourselves. Stand still and see the salvation of the Lord" (Isa. 54:17; 2 Chron. 20:15; Exod. 14:13).

A "but" crops up into the board meeting, and you say, "Is anything too hard for God?" Kick "but!" You can't seem to get out of bed, kick "but," for in him we live, and move, and have our very being.

Kick. "God is good and is ready to forgive and plenteous in mercy unto all who call." Kick. "The voice of God is powerful." Kick. "Be strong and courageous. Be not afraid." Kick. "All things work together for good." Kick. "Being confident of this very thing, that he which hath begun a good work in you will complete it." Kick. "God is able." Kick. "I can do all things through Christ who strengthens me." Kick. "God will fight your battles."

How to survive the jungle? Fight back with the word of God. Kick "but!"

THE WORD

But I did not do so, because of the fear of God. Indeed, I devoted myself to the work on this wall. . . . "

—Nehemiah 5:15–16

The Right Stuff

Have you ever said, "I just can't wait until the day?" You utter the statement filled with hope and longing as you peer beyond the present horizon to events that lie ahead. As much as life demands from your present day, there is an impatience to move to the next rung of living. You get a good case of the "I just can't waits."

I can't wait until . . . I get a promotion or a raise. I can tell my coworkers where to go and retire. I can send my children off to college. I can send my grandchildren back to live with their parents. I can pay off the mortgage or the car note. I can write a check that won't bounce. I can get a new job. I can empty my nest, take care of my needs, clean up my own mess, hit big at bingo, follow my dreams, and ride off into the sunset with the love of my life. I just can't wait. I just can't wait . . . until my lonely is not so lonely, relief is in sight, the cavalry shows up, go on a real vacation, get a real woman, get a real man, my prayers are answered, my ship comes in, make it to the top, have it made, and possess my success.

If we could ask Nehemiah that question, I wonder what he would say. Perhaps he would say, "I just couldn't wait until all ten gates of the cities are completed: The Sheep Gate, the Fish Gate, the Old Gate, the Valley Gate, the Dung Gate, the Water Gate, the Gate of Foundation, the East Gate, House Gate, and Gate MathCAD. I can't wait until the breach has been completed in the wall, the farmers return to their fields, apothecaries to their medicine, goldsmiths to their crafts, mothers to their children, when we can put down sword and spear, and lay down the trowel behind a restored wall of protection to the glory of God!"

The story of the king's cupbearer in Babylon, now the builder and leader of liberation in Jerusalem, is unfolding. The primacy of prayer was a prelude to action in the first chapter. Prayer has given way to the work on the wall in Jerusalem.

Nehemiah moved beyond the first round of opposition from Sanballat, Tobiah and Geshem. They were the enemies without. This "new pastor" of the Jerusalem assembly is now having internal problems, the enemies within. The people who did not have the wealth to provide for their families borrowed heavily to obtain necessities. The rich took advantage of the situation and charged interest. Hurting families mortgaged land if they had any or sold their children into bondage to satisfy the debts they could not pay.

An angry Nehemiah confronts the problem without affixing blame. A covenant is signed to prevent future financially abusive behavior. He now stops the work so that the people can heal. However, a funny thing happened on the way to completing the wall. Nehemiah was promoted (Neh. 5:14).

He was not just God's builder anymore. He was the governor of Jerusalem serving for twelve years. His leadership star rose quickly. In the midst of the problems was a promotion. He found success working on the wall.

Life is like that sometimes, on your way to your destiny God gives an unexpected blessing. While you are "waiting until the day," God elevates you. Many times it is not handling opposition, but handling success that trips up a leader. How did Nehemiah handle his promotion? There are many sermons preached to help people cope in a crisis. Bible studies are taught to help people survive under stress and advance in their adversities.

Songs are sung about coping and adaptive strategies, "Climbing up the Rough Side of the Mountain," "Lord Help Me to Hold Out," "Hold Back the Night," "Everything Is Going to be Alright," and "Hold to God's Unchanging Hand." Or sing Donny McClurkin's, "We Fall Down, but We Get Up."

We do not spend a lot of time preaching sermons and singing

songs, helping people to handle success while handling distress, helping people to handle their promotions before the promotion handles them.

Many people perish in the jungle world of work, not because it was too hot and too hard, but because they fainted in the lime-light of success. Success can aggravate ones weaknesses and short-comings. Notoriety may cause some people to lose their identity. The public persona takes precedence over the private persona.

When the external excitement of the promotion wanes, there are those who lose sight of priorities and values. They seek to regain the intoxicating, addictive "fifteen minutes of fame." We do not need to look far down the annals of fortune and fame to see who stumbled over the hurdles of success. The annals of history are prevalent with personalities who could handle the rough road to success but not the trips and trappings of success.

Many men and women have lamented, after they have lost their souls and identities to the bright light of success, that the happiest moments were in the days of struggle, when no one clamored for autographs, and the media didn't know their names.

It is often in the excitement of a promotion that many lose sight of what is important and valuable. Some spend money as fast as they make it. Others self-destruct, drunk on its intoxicating power. Success sometimes "goes to their head"; people forget where they came from and who their real friends are. Success can propel you to a different economic neighborhood where some people are uncomfortable. They never entirely leave the old neighborhood and some-times their old ways catch up with them, as they did with the late Tupac Shakur and the late Christopher Wallace, a.k.a. Biggie Smalls.

Howard Hughes died a recluse. Toni Braxton reportedly went bankrupt. Joe Johnson died a broken man. Billie Holliday over-dosed. Marilyn Monroe took her own life. Michael Jackson seems to try to recapture his childhood through "Never Land."

How did Nehemiah handle the greater success gained on the road to victory? There are certain common characteristics with every promotion. There are new responsibilities. The buck no longer stops at someone else's desk. It stops at yours. There are new tasks to learn and proficiencies to acquire.

The rules of relationship may change as one moves up the leadership ladder. Interaction with the vice president is ultimately different from that of the chairperson of the board of directors. People respond differently to you. There is one level of relationship between coworkers, when you were all a part of the management team. There is another when you are promoted to be in charge of the management team.

Your decisions have a greater impact upon people. In your former capacity, what you did may have influenced a few people. Promotion increases the impact of your success and failure on others. One wrong move could cost the livelihoods of many employees and their families.

Promotion increases your visibility. What you think, say, and do is now up to public scrutiny. Private becomes public quickly. It is as if the whole world is watching your every move as you take the reigns of your new assignment.

Your opinion will be sought after. Where you stand on issues will signal others to take the same or opposite stand. Your favor will be courted and many times your integrity corrupted.

New privileges come with promotions. There may be an expense account, company car, a key to the executive washroom, a parking space, membership in private or business clubs, a secretary, larger office space, your own budget, staff, retirement, or health benefit package. In Nehemiah's case, new privileges came with his promotion, too. There was food allotted for the governor, and money allowed for his household expenses.

New policies come with promotions. You become privy to the policies and procedures of previous administrations. There is an expectation that you will continue in certain traditions and favors granted from those who have held your position.

In the past, governors took forty shekels and bread and wine from the people. Their servants pressured the people to give all they could. His predecessors took advantage of their position and purchased land for themselves.

Nehemiah indicates that he will not go the way of his predecessors and oppress the people. The fear of God restrains him from continuing the abusive policies. "I did not demand the food allowance of the governor, because of the heavy burden of labor on the people" (Neh. 5:18).

More than one hundred-fifty people ate at the governor's table daily. Officials, Jews, and others came from the surrounding nations to Nehemiah's daily dinner table. As a host, he was responsible to feed them. He was building the walls, a governor for the people, and handling popularity by not overburdening the people under his authority.

As the new kid on the block, you will have an opportunity to continue policies or begin new ones. You can misuse your new position perpetuating injustices. Or you can act with integrity. The mistake many new leaders make is that because someone else did it and got away with it, then they can do the same. They feel a sense of entitlement, often allowing their proclivities to get in the way of production and performance.

Your service record will not be judged because of the past policies of your predecessors, but upon the character you demonstrate in your position. How did Nehemiah handle his promotion? He did not abuse privilege and power. He properly interpreted policies. He refused to inherit the inappropriate policies of his predecessors. He had a genuine concern for the people and the project.

Nehemiah's secret to success was a vibrant relationship with God. God was his anchor in the shifting sands of leadership. His relationship was so unshakable that he was not wooed with favors, money, and provision. Maybe Nehemiah knew that the God who can get you to the top is also the God who can keep you on top. In the end, Nehemiah prayed, "Remember for my good, O my God, all that I have done for this people" (Neh. 5:19). The higher you go up the ladder of success, the deeper you need to go in prayer. Nehemiah started out praying and continued to pray as governor.

Many of our battles are fought and won on our knees before

rush hour traffic and staff meetings. It is in prayer that God guides and gives direction to our destiny. It is in prayer that the Spirit whispers to our tired minds and body, "So let us not grow weary in doing what is right, for we will reap at harvest time, if we do not give up" (Gal. 6:9). It is in prayer that we are encouraged to fight on. "Weeping may linger for a night, but joy comes with the morning" (Ps. 30:5). It is in prayer that the impossibilities become possible because "... nothing will be impossible with God" (Luke 1:37). It is in prayer that "In my distress I cry to the Lord, that he may answer me" (Ps. 120:1). In prayer our hearts are encouraged; "When evildoers assail me to devour my flesh—my adversaries and foes—they shall stumble and fall" (Ps. 27:2). Nehemiah had the right stuff. He had a heart for God and a mind to work.

THE WORD

So I sent messengers to them, saying, "I am doing a great work and I cannot come down. Why should the work stop while I leave it to come down to you?"—Nehemiah 6:3

It's a Love Thing, You Ought to Understand

There is such a thing as a problem with tenure. Have you ever had a problem that has lasted a long time? These are not problems that are momentary inconveniences that are here today and gone tomorrow. They are not those brief touches with travesty, tragedy, and turmoil. Everyone has had a problem or two, and you still have this one problem with tenure. Others have moved on to their third or fourth problem and you are still wrestling with the same problem. Testimonies have been given about problems solved, but you are held captive by this one long-term problem. Many have prayed and received their answers. Fasting has brought relief. Yet, you are still worrying heaven about the same problem with tenure.

If you think you have had a long-term problem, talk to the woman with the issue of blood. Her problem lasted so long that both the money and the physician ran out. Speak with Hannah. Everyone was having babies but her. Spend time with the man by the Pool of Bethesda. He had a problem that lasted thirty-eight years.

Have a conversation with Moses. He had a forty-year problem in the wilderness. Paul and Silas had a problem locked in a Roman jail. Daniel had a problem in a den of lions. Jesus had a problem on a cross. Nehemiah had a problem trying to rebuild the wall of Jerusalem. In the sixth chapter of Nehemiah, Nehemiah is working on a problem with tenure, Sanballat, Tobiah, and Geshem.

The history of this writing appears to be well-established with the discovery of ancient evidence, such as the *Elephantine Papyri*. Artaxerxes 1 was the authoritative leader, the son of Xerxes, the king who took Esther to be his queen.

The book covers a period of approximately twenty years. It shows that both Ezra's and Nehemiah's work overlapped (Neh. 8:1–9; 12:26). Some scholars believe that Malachi also prophesied during Nehemiah's term as governor.

The narrative is written in first person singular along with a few third person exceptions. It shows Nehemiah to be a resourceful and courageous leader. He had been faithful to the law of God and was determined to rebuild the wall.

The security of the city depended upon the strength of the walls. Some scholars contend that the walls were preparation for a greater task, rebuilding the temple. Nehemiah was bringing about revival, not just rebuilding.

The opposition to rebuilding the walls was present before Nehemiah arrived from Babylon. Leaders are confronted with problems that were there before they arrive and may be there long after their departure.

There are some problems that refuse to go away. They go into hiding like snipers in the bush or Klingons on a reconnaissance mission invisible because of a cloaking device. The work on the wall was progressing. The gaping holes were being filled in. The city would no longer be vulnerable to an open attack. They would have a defense again marauding armies, wild animals, and enemies seeking to conquer new territory.

When walls are not secure, the community is defenseless. The walls of our modern day community are family, school, and church. When these institutions become vulnerable, crumble and fall, enemies destroy the fabric and quality of life. We need modern-day Nehemiahs who are willing to stand up to those who would erode the strength and security of our communities!

The building of the wall progressed and victory seemed assured. A message comes from the opposition. Tobiah was married into a prominent Jewish family. He had contact with many persons in Judah who could feed him information about the work Nehemiah was doing. Some of his acquaintances worked as antagonists and spies.

Sanballat and Geshem try to lure Nehemiah to a meeting. The invitation to Ono, on the Plain of Sharon, outside of the city was to discuss mutual community interests. It sounded innocent enough. Nehemiah refused to meet with them. He concluded that the work was so important that he could not afford to stop now. "Why should the work stop while I leave it to come down to you?"(Neh. 6:3).

The problem with these three was not settled when the work originally began; it continued even through the final phase of renovation. Nehemiah did not allow the problem to distract him from his assignment. Problems with tenure may not stop the progress of your work, but they will try to distract you.

Four times the messenger came and four times the message was sent back by Nehemiah (Neh. 6:4). The same response was given again and again by the governor of Jerusalem. The constant distractions were a tactic of Sanballat and Geshem to discourage Nehemiah. When the enemy cannot divert your attention, it will try to put a damper on things.

When there is always a fire to put out in the kitchen, you can get tired of hauling water. If there is always a lot of murmuring, bickering, infighting, haggling, and arguments, it can be depressing. When strikes threaten to close you down, or work slowdowns impede progress, it can be disheartening. Ambushes disguised as meetings and unnecessary conferences can be discouraging. Constant and consistent confrontation can wear you down.

Nehemiah's problem with a tenure changed tactics (Neh. 6:5). They sent an unsealed, open message accusing Nehemiah of planning a rebellion against the king. He was falsely condemned for appointing prophets to announce to Jerusalem that he is king.

This kind of letter was a public missive, read and examined by others. The problem now moved from private to public confrontation. If they could have stopped Nehemiah, they would have a long time ago. Since distraction and discouragement did not work, they tried to distort the reason for the rebuilding effort. The project was not for communal gain, but for personal promotion.

Nehemiah responded that there was no such rumor going around town. The only gossip was that which Sanballat, Tobiah, and Geshem created. The fear of public condemnation would weaken their efforts, but Nehemiah prayed and God strengthened their hands (Neh. 6:9). Again the opposition moved. At the house of Shemaiah, who was probably a priest, Nehemiah was asked to meet in the house of God. Shemaiah advised him that men were coming to kill him by night and he needed protection. The best place to hide was in the sacredness of the sanctuary. The opposition was encouraging him to destroy himself. Sometimes the press of problems will make you do things against your own better judgment. The sheer weight of the pressure is designed so that you turn on yourself. They cannot stop you, so they try to get you to stop yourself.

Nehemiah saw through this ruse. He refused to go into the temple because he was not a priest and would not violate the temple by entering inside. He also did not want to put his safety above the safety of those who worked with him on the wall.

How did Nehemiah handle problems with tenure? How do we handle our own? First of all, Nehemiah trusted God. Problems may come and go, or stay for a long time, but you can trust God not to forsake the righteous or allow his seed to beg bread.

The writer in Proverbs says, "Trust in the Lord with all your heart, and do not rely on your own insight" (Prov. 3:5–6). Job states, "Though he slay me, yet will I trust him" (Job 13:15). The hymn writer sings, "I will trust in the Lord until I die." The best way to handle problems with tenure is to trust God for the outcome. Trust God with your past, present, and future.

Sometimes it may look like things are not going to work out. Trust God anyhow. Things may not be going your way. Trust God anyhow. Problems are consistent burdens hampering the forward progress of your work. Trust God anyhow. No matter how hard you work, problems will not go away. Trust God anyhow.

Secondly, Nehemiah stayed with God's plan. In the very beginning, Nehemiah prayed to God for four months. God granted him favor before the king. God gave him provision and protection. God revealed the tricks of the enemy. God gave him the ability to gain a consensus and a following. God promoted him. God was Nehemiah's guiding force. Why change horses in the middle of the river?

His antagonists messed with him, messed over him, and tried to mess him up. Nehemiah did not change his game plan. He did not play the game by the rules of the opposition. He did not adopt their tactics of threats, intimidation, and violence. He simply followed the leading of the Lord, and it worked! Nehemiah kept on working, building, fixing, managing, caring, serving, and so must you.

Lastly, Nehemiah loved God. God loves us. God then calls us to love each other. We are not to love each other with our own fragile human love. But we are to love with a love that comes from loving God with all of our heart, mind, and soul. This love demands total participation from our heart, mind, and soul. It helps us to see each other in a new perspective, with eyes of love. Thus we can love our neighbor as ourselves, pray for those who despitefully use us, do good to those who hate us, and love even our enemies.

Nehemiah loved God, and there is nothing more powerful than a man or woman who loves God. It was his love for God that kept him in a broken-down city, trying to correct family relationships and usher in the season of revival.

You will not be able to make it in the jungle of the world of work where only the strong survives without the love of God. How do you survive in the jungle? It is a love thing, and you ought to understand.

Let us return to the beginning. There are problems with tenure. Remember Hannah? She had a baby one year after leaving the temple. Remember the woman with the issue of blood? The blood dried up. Remember the man by the Pool of Bethesda? He got up. Remember the bent over women? She got up. Remember Moses? He saw the Promised Land. Remember Daniel? He is no longer in the lions den. Remember Paul and Silas? They got out of jail. Remember Jesus? He got up with all power in his hands!

"I was sinking deep in sin, far from the peaceful shores. Very deeply strained within, sinking to rise no more. But the master of the sea heard my disparaging cry. From the waters lifted me now safe am I. Love lifted me. Love lifted me. When nothing else can help. Love lifted me."[3]

Survival in the jungle requires trusting, staying with God's plan for your life, and love of God and each other. It is a love thing and you ought to understand.

Chapter five

Living beyond the Stereotypes

ॐ

SOME HURDLES THAT women who happen to be leaders face are stereotypes—the group of fixed notions about a person or groups of persons, or the conceptions that surround a position or occupation. There are stereotypes about certain ethnic, social, cultural, or religious organizations. There are stereotypes surrounding Christians, Jews, Muslims, and Buddhists. There are stereotypes about people of African, Polish, Irish, or Hispanic descent.

There are also stereotypes that face women in leadership positions. There is the bun in the hair, Red-Cross-shoe-wearing preacher. The witch on a broom, and the sleep-your-way-to-the-top-vixen stereotype of an executive officer is another one. There is the no-life-of-your-own single leader, and the cry-when-it-doesn't-go-your-way weepy leader.

A man may be viewed as confident, but a woman with similar actions is sometimes stereotyped as an arrogant, pushy broad. A man may be viewed as a strong commanding leader, but women are often stereotyped as something related to a female dog.

Society has used stereotypes historically to exclude persons from certain mainstream positions of power, according to Patricia Reid-Merritt in *Sister Power*.[1] They have been used to keep people in a perceived place that was acceptable to the majority group. They were used to keep others "in line." Stereotypes are a part of our existence. They can be both positive and negative. They can also become self-fulfilling prophecies.

How do you live beyond the stereotypes that have been assigned to you, your history, heritage, gender, or ethnic origin? This sermon, "Living beyond Your Stereotypes," may help answer the question.

THE WORD

The next day Jesus decided to go to Galilee. He found Philip and said to him, "Follow me." Now Philip was from Bethsaida, the city of Andrew and Peter. Philip found Nathanael and said to him, "We have found him about whom Moses in the Law, and also the prophets wrote, Jesus son of Joseph from Nazareth." Nathanael said to him, "Can anything good come out of Nazareth?" Philip said to him, "Come and see." When Jesus saw Nathanael coming toward him, he said to him, "Here is truly an Israelite in whom there is no deceit!"—John 1:43–47

Living beyond Your Stereotypes

Let us take a true-and-false quiz today. A scenario will be presented, and you can answer true or false. Raise your hand, nod your head, say amen, or shout hallelujah at the appropriate moment. Ready?

All women of African descent are Jezebels, witches, and whores. Is it true or false? All men of African descent are violent. Is it true or false? All people of African descent can sing and dance. Is it true or false? All persons of African descent have rhythm. Is it true or false?

Persons of African descent have athletic prowess that is unsurpassed by any other ethnic group in the world. Is that true or false? Black people do not play tennis, golf, chess, or ballroom dance. Is this true or false?

All African American young men have a criminal record. Is this true or false? They are all on crack cocaine or other addictive substances. They all beat and cheat on their women. Is this true or false?

All young girls of African descent are pregnant before sixteen years of age. They all have big hips, big lips, and big attitudes. Is it true or false?

All people of African descent are lazy, can't be trusted, and are con artists, burglars, and carjackers. They are oversexed and uneducated and unemployed by choice. They are bad risks and good dressers and dancers. They all like fried chicken, pigs feet, chitterlings, and collard greens. They speak broken English, live in broken down houses, and are products of broken relationships. They are to blame for their own second-class citizenship. Just like Bebe's kids, they do not die. They just multiply. Is this true or false?

If you answered true to any of the statements, you have bought into the stereotypes that have been assigned to men and women of African descent. These thoughts are nothing new. Ask the eldest among us and they have probably heard all of these statements before. These stereotypes have been promoted in various art forms from *Uncle Tom's Cabin* to *Gone with the Wind*.

In the environment in which we live, there exists a simplified conception of who we are and what we do. There is a standardized image that ignores individual characteristics. It ignores the diversity among us from skin color to culinary tastes. It eschews originality and cast-types us all in certain categories from which it seems impossible to escape.

Dr. Ernest Johnson, in *Brothers on the Mend*, writes about many incidents that are reflective of stereotypes. Newspaper headlines report on the injustices, and television newscasts perpetuate them. People stopped and searched by law enforcement agents for no other reason than that they fit the profile or stereotype. People stopped by police because they looked like they did not belong in a certain neighborhood because they fit the profile. A man handcuffed in front of his neighbors and forced to walk room to room in his own home. The crime?—he was without identification in a neighborhood that did not fit the stereotype.

A mother blames a nonexistent black man for kidnapping her two children and drowning them in a lake. A man falsely accuses a nonexistent black man for the murder of his pregnant wife. It was all done to cover their own crimes. Yet, because they fit the violent-crime stereotype, many people were all-too-willing to believe it to be true as law enforcement agencies searched for them. It fit the stereotype.

Stereotypes have a mean way of stripping away a person's dignity. They march over your self-esteem, ripping it to shreds with their prejudicial combat boots of fear and rage. Stereotypes fix in the mind of a community commonly-held beliefs that may or may not be true. They may be fair or unfair, earned or unearned, beliefs about a person or groups of persons.

Stereotypes find expression in the places where we work. Instead of getting to know someone, stereotypes have already colored expectations. They come between coworkers with a mindset of definitions. Instead of judging someone on their merits, stereotypes may even color opinion.

Stereotypes live in our homes. They are a part of our relationships with the opposite sex. It is sometimes easier to believe a stereotype than it is to appreciate someone's uniqueness. They are also taught consciously or unconsciously to our children.

There are times when we take out our frustrations of living under the burden of stereotypes with each other. We use substances to cope with the negativity that stereotypes produce. We blame each other and other ethnic groups for our problems living with the residue of stereotypes in our lives. We bury the angry and hurt feelings that the pain the profiling causes. We try to deny its existence by believing we do not belong to the group that is negatively stereotyped. We try to pretend that the stereotypes do not affect us, or we join the other side of society and lash out at our brothers and sisters for living the stereotype rather than living beyond it.

It is not just women of African descent; we all have stereotypes to deal with. There is the stereotype of the black preacher typified in television situation comedies such as "Amen" and "Good Times." There is the stereotyped deacon played by Sherman Hemsley. Ethel Waters and Butterfly McQueen were the mammies of early motion pictures. Lena Horne's Sweet Georgia Brown was the stereotypical Jezebel. Stepin' Fetchit typified the black man in Jim Crow American life like the characters George Jefferson and Martin add to the stereotypes of today. Buckwheat was the stereotypical black child of the 1930s and 1940s. Urkle and Moesha are the typified images of black youth today.

There was Dianne Carol's "Julia" in the 1960s, and later, Esther Rolle's "Florida" as typifying single black parents on television. In this decade, we have Monique as the single mother on "The Parkers."

The Huxtables' middle-class, two-parent family life spoke volumes against the stereotyped families of African descent who are always broken and female-led. It portrayed a couple trying to raise their children that presented a view opposite the belief by some that we are unable to raise our own children, as seen in such shows as "Webster" or "Different Stokes." The working class family image of "Roc" took another swing at stereotypes with its working-class, extended family unit. We all have stereotypes that face us on a daily basis. A stereotype is no respecter of either gender, ethnic, religious, or socioeconomic group.

How do you live beyond the stereotypes that follow closely like a shadow cast by the noonday sun? How do you live with what they say you are or want you to be, especially when you know you are not like and do not want to be like that? How do you break the mold society has cast for you and your community?

Stereotypes are so insidious that they can become self-fulfilling prophecies. If enough people say it is true, than many conclude that it must be true. If it is true, then I must be like that since it is what the world expects me to be. It may be too hard to do or be anything else. You're trying to sing "Young, Gifted, and Black" when society is singing "Young, Gangster, and Rap." You're trying to go to college while everyone wants to know about the stereotypical thug life. You're just trying to do your job efficiently and the fear of a neomatriarchy keeps you in the secretarial pool.

The hymnologist writes, "Jesus knows all about our troubles. He will strive till the day is done. There's not a friend like the lowly Jesus, No not one. No, not one."[2] I am glad for a savior who knows what we are going through. Jesus dealt with stereotypes as a Jew, a carpenter from Nazareth, and as the Son of God.

The beginning of John's gospel gives the prelude to the earthly ministry of Jesus. John unfolds it by a poetic piece that celebrates Jesus' oneness with the Father and His coming into the world as the Word made flesh. Then this biographer adds the witness of John the Baptist and this pericope in verses 43–47, presenting the gathering of the first disciples.

The Baptist sees Jesus coming towards him and affirms his divinity by calling him the Lamb of God who takes away the sins of the world. This expression may be reflective of a sacrifice in general. It seems to announce that this is the sacrifice that would atone for the world's sin.

The next day, two of John's disciples inquired about where Jesus was staying. They followed him and spent the day with him. One of the two, Andrew, went to his brother announcing, "We have found the Messiah." He brought his brother to Jesus. The next day, as Jesus decided to leave, Philip finds his brother and brings him to Jesus.

Each brother was compelled to reach for another. Neither was content to dominate the Lord's time. They shared their new discovery; this is the long awaited messiah. This is the one that Moses wrote would come. This is the sacrifice that would satisfy the sin-debt we owe. Come and see. Like children over a new toy or found buried treasure, they wanted to share the good news.

We must continue the example of these brothers. Each person reaching out to tell others that Jesus is here. We must continue to reach others for Jesus Christ. We must never be so satisfied with Jesus for ourselves that we make church our exclusive property as though it were a country club or private supper club. Once you have found him, share him. When you are converted, my brother and sister, declares the Word of God, strengthen one another (Luke 22:32). Jesus immediately renames Simon, son of John, to Cephas or Peter. His new title, meaning "rock" or "stone," refers more to what Peter was to become rather than who he was. Peter was impetuous and unstable. Yet, when others said that Jesus was John the Baptist or Isaiah, Peter would declare that Jesus is the Christ, the son of the living God.

He would become the Lord's garden defender. He would brag about his loyalty, but would deny him in the midnight hour before the cocked crowed thrice. Yet, he would become the Pentecost preacher leading thousands to a relationship in Jesus Christ.

Jesus was not hindered by his present condition. He looked beyond his faults to a time of transformation in the future. His present state did not eliminate him from service. His past did not exempt from blessings or being a blessing.

It is a reminder that our present condition is a transitory circumstance to what we can become. Jesus looks at our becoming. He doesn't put a period where a comma can go. The next day, Jesus finds Philip and issues an invitation to follow him. Andrew and Peter were from the city of Bethsaida. This was a large city on the north shore of the Galilee near the Jordan River, whose name meant "house of fishing."

Philip finds his brother Nathanael to tell him Jesus is the fulfiller of the prophecies of a coming Messiah. He identifies not as the Son of God, the Christos, but by earthly identification. This Jesus of Nazareth, the son of Joseph.

"Nazareth!" declares Nathanael. "Can anything good come from there?" Nathanael had never seen Jesus. He did not know Jesus. He did not know Jesus' family. He was not privy to the uniqueness of his gifts and skills. He had never come within his circle of influence. He had no concrete information beyond his brother's testimony. He had already made up his mind about who this Jesus was. His belief about all those who come from Nazareth tainted the meeting that was to take place.

How many times have we made up our minds about someone even before we are introduced based on the color of their skin, their heritage, personal history, their bank account, the expense of the wardrobe, or their standard of living? All Nathanael had beyond a family notation was a location. This was the stop side at the crossroads of life and conversion.

Stereotyped. Even Jesus could not escape a prejudicial opinion. "He came to what was his own, and his own people did not accept him" (John 1:11). Nothing good comes out of Nazareth so how could this be the Messiah when everyone knows about those people in that city?

Nazareth has been described as a frontier town. It is located on the southern border of Zebulun out of the mainstream of Jewish life. That may have fostered a certain aloofness. It was being located close to trade routes that brought them into constant contact with other people from other countries. The inhabitants of Nazareth were said to speak a ruder dialect. They were considered less cultured and civilized.

Nathanael had contempt for people who didn't talk like everyone else. He had contempt for their downtown aspect in his uptown world. We tend to do the same thing. People who we consider less than, we hold in contempt. If they do not shop, work, or live at our perceived level, we do tend to look down our noses at those people.

It is amazing how we stereotype each other and allow this mindset to keep us from getting acquainted. Think of all the friendships never made because of someone else's idea about the haves and the have-nots, the educated and the uneducated, the erudite and the dropout, the crude and rude with the Emily Posts of the world. It is amazing what we allow to separate us without taking the time to discover for ourselves. We simply make up our minds about someone based upon superficial observations. Our idea of someone is based on stale assumptions passed on to you by someone else. How did Jesus live beyond the stereotypes?

Philip's response did not play into Nathanael's preconceived notion about Jesus. He did not try to defend Jesus. He did not issue an extensive dissertation about the Messiah. He did not offer excuses or words of condemnation about Nathanael's hasty conclusion. Philip simply said, "Come and see."

The best destroyer of stereotypes is knowledge to the contrary. It is coming close enough for you to see. Developing your own opinion, not based on someone else's assumption, but upon personal knowledge.

Is there any such thing as all men are, all women are, all persons of African descent are, all Polish people are, all Hispanics are, and all Asians are? All husbands are and all wives are? We hastily assign general conclusions to individual, personal, uniquenesses. Come and see! How did Jesus live beyond the stereotypes?

Know Who You Are

John records that Nicodemus, a member of the Jewish ruling council, came to inquire about the identity of Jesus (John 3:2). John the Baptist sent his disciples to see if Jesus was the Christ or should they look for another (Matt. 11:2–3).

The people in Jerusalem wondered who was this Man. "Can it be that the authorities really know that this is the Messiah?" (John 7:26). Others said, "This is the Messiah," but some asked, "Surely the Messiah does not come from Galilee, does he?" (John 7:41).

The religious establishment confronted and challenged who he was and whose he was. Pilate asks, "Are you the King of the Jews?" (John 18:33). Jesus questions his disciples, "Who do people say that the Son of Man is?" (Matt. 16:13).

Jesus knew who he was. The Jews claimed he was demon-possessed (John 8:48). He was not the product of public opinion on erroneous assumptions. He was not trying to be the John the Baptist some thought him to be, or the Elijah others believed. This did not trap him. Just because they were saying it, didn't make it true.

All through John's gospel, Jesus is clear about who he is. I am the bread of life. I am the living bread. The Jewish ancestors ate manna, bread from heaven, and still died. Eat the bread living of Christ and live forever.

Jesus said, "I am the light of the world. Whoever follows me will never walk in darkness but will have the light of life" (John 8:12). He was certain of his identify and declared, "I am the gate . . . whoever enters by me will be saved . . . I am the good shepherd. The good shepherd lays down his life for the sheep" (John 10:7–16).

Others may have been confused, but Jesus was not. To Martha standing before Lazarus's tomb, "I am the resurrection and the life" (John 11:25). Thomas was unsure about direction and Jesus responds, "I am the way and the truth and the life" (John 14:5–7). "I am the true vine and my Father is the gardener" (John 15:1).

Jesus did not believe the stereotype because he knew exactly who he was. We cannot afford to live beneath our potential in Jesus Christ by living according to stereotype. We need to remind ourselves on a regular basis that we are children of the King. We are a peculiar people fearfully and wonderfully made. We are the elect. We are the chosen seed. We are royal priesthood, a holy nation, belonging to God. We are children of the light no longer of the darkness. We are more than conquerors. We were created in the image of God to show forth His praises. Mankind may reject us, but just like Jesus, God chooses us.

Jesus Understood His Mission

Jesus came as the sacrificial Lamb of God to take away the world's sin. Everyone seemed to have an idea about what he was supposed to do and when he was supposed to do it. Mary wanted him to fix a social blunder by solving the wine problem at a wedding in Cana. "Woman, what concern is that to you and to me?" Jesus replied, "My hour has not yet come" (John 2:1–5). After feeding five thousand men, along with countless women and children, they intended to take him by force and make him king. He had to withdraw from a mountain by himself (John 6:15).

Jesus knew that his realm was not of this world. On trial before Pilate, Pilate asked him, "So you are a king?" Jesus answered, "You say that I am a king. For this I was born, and for this I came into the world, to testify to the truth" (John 18:37).

He methodically prepared his disciples for his eminent sacrifice. He worked many miracles; explained about the other counselor, the Holy Spirit to come; demonstrated the example of love; gave new commandments; all the while preparing them, as he himself prepared to go to prepare a place for them.

Jesus understood His mission. He was not sidetracked by other misconceptions and neither must we be. You will find a lot of people who have an idea about what you can and cannot do. It is best to receive your marching orders from God. There are those who may tell you women cannot do certain things. Women are not emotionally suited for certain tasks. They are not physically able to do some things.

When I was in junior high school, which tells you how long it has been since I was in what is called middle school, people had peculiar ideas about girl's sports. Basketball was only played half-court. You could only dribble twice and then you had to shoot. Girls were excused from physical exercise on certain days of the month. Today, young women enjoy a full spectrum of team and individual sports. They excel in full court basketball and, praise God, have their own WNBA professional league. We have come a long way.

Some people will ascribe certain stereotypical behaviors to your ethnic group. Some will have lower expectations because of the stereotypes they have about "you people" who come from communities of contempt. Some may push you into activities based on stereotypes such as: if you are Asian, you must own a restaurant or play the violin; if you are of Indian extraction, you must become a shopkeeper; if you are of African descent, you may play a team sport.

Angel Graham's parents listened to her high school counselor suggest vocational training over a college education. Angel was in a college preparatory curriculum. She had respectable grades. She was active in the life of the school. But during the early days of integration, many of the students of African decent were advised to do anything but go to college in spite of their obvious qualifications.

You must be clear about your own destination. You must have a sense of the mission that God has set aside for all who are ambassadors of Jesus Christ. You are not bound and duty to live your life according to someone else's stereotype. God calls. God sends. God equips. God prepares. God sustains. God empowers. It is best to listen to God and turn the volume down on the world's stereotypes.

In It but Not of It

Nazareth had a less than desirable reputation. Its ugly stereotype stood between Jesus and those who believed nothing good could come out of that neighborhood. He came from a town where the people were characterized as perhaps mean, insignificant, and uncultured. Yet, its crude rudeness was not a part of him.

He lived in its mess. He was not part of the mess. He lived in a hostile environment, but he was not touched by its meanness. He started out in a hard place, but ended up seated on the right hand of God. He started out in a barn, and ended up in glory. Who cares where you come from when it's where you end up that counts?

He was wrongly accused, misunderstood, and misinterpreted; yet he remained clear about whom he was and the nature of his mission. He lived beyond the stereotypes. He lived beyond their made-up minds with a shout, "I have conquered the world" (John 16:33).

How do you live beyond the stereotypes? Just follow Jesus. Know who you are and live up to it! Understand God's mission and work it! You may be a card-carrying, bonified, qualified, identified member of Stereotype Land, but you don't have to live up to false notions. The best weapon against stereotype is to extend Philip's invitation Come and see. Come and see.

Chapter six

When Someone Needs Help

❧

EVERY LEADER NEEDS help sometimes. We've all needed a favor, a word spoken on our behalf or a second chance.

We've needed to borrow something, an idea, staff support, budget analysis, copier, cell phone, or money. Maybe there was the need for a place to stay, a refuge, a hideout, or a hangout. Help to complete an assignment; finish a major research paper; get the job done; get a resume through the review stage; or get in touch with the right people.

Every leader needs help once in a while. We need help to think through a problem, talk through a situation, or just hear ourselves think out loud. We need help to get a job or keep a job, get a raise, a promotion, or a favorable performance review. We need help with a question, search for an answer, find our way through life, or have common misconceptions clarified. Every leader needs help. Help to practice until it's perfect or prepare properly for a board of directors' presentation. We need help to ask until it's given to us. We need help to seek until it's found and knock until doors open (Matt. 7:7).

We need help during times of difficulty. Help to forgive friends and enemies, to turn the other cheek, return good for evil. Help to see the good in the worst of us and make the best of bad situations. Help! Everybody needs it sometimes. Help to stand on your own two feet, to wait until things work out, or to start over again and again and again. Help to hold on in a storm, to do what you have never done, to be what you want to be. Most of us declare that we can use financial help. Help with debt-free living, balancing the checkbook, or increasing a Wall Street portfolio.

We could use help around the house, with babysitting, and strategic child maintenance. Help with aging parents. We need exercise help. Dieting help. Workout help. Wardrobe help. Help making it from day to day.

It would be hard to find a leader who has never needed help. We all need help every now and then. No matter how bright, smart, articulate, self sufficient, and proficient a personality may be, we all need help along the way.

It does not matter how many degrees hang on your wall, the high price tags on the clothes hanging in your closet, or the amount of cash stashed away, we all need help every now and then. No matter how strong the body, how sincere the effort, how brilliant the mind, we all need help in our lives.

Leaders need help. Title, authority, or executive privilege does not exempt you from needing help.

Nehemiah needed help to rebuild Jerusalem. Elijah needed the help of a widow's flour and oil to stay alive.

Lot needed help to leave Sodom and Gomorrah. Rehab needed help to get out of a suspicious lifestyle. Sarah needed help to get out of Pharaoh's harem. The woman caught in adultery needed the help of a forgiving savior.

The woman with the issue of blood needed healing help. Paul and Silas needed help to get out of a Roman jail. Martha needed Mary's help in the kitchen.

The thief hanging on a cross wanted help. He wanted Jesus to remember him when he came into his realm. Jesus needed help to carry his cross up Calvary Hill! Every leader needs help sometimes.

There are many ways to respond when someone needs help. It could take the form of direct application of resources, personal intervention, wise counsel, referral, or instruction. Good athletes benefit from coaches. Leaders benefit from mentors.

In the ancient Greek story "The Odyssey," Mentor is the name of a trusted friend. In Ulysses's absence, Mentor educates, nurtures, protects, and guides his son Telemochees into adulthood. He is described as an old man, a shepherd of the people, who is often impersonated by the goddess Athena.

The attributes of God reflect the functionalities of a mentor. God as parent is a counselor, guide, teacher, and liberator who becomes incarnate through Jesus Christ. Jesus teaches us about God's care and our responsibility to each other.

Jesus is a mentor, teacher, and rabbi. He reminds his mentees who they are (Matt. 5:13–16). He calls them his friends. He shows them what to do, demonstrates it for them, and then commissions them to do the same (Matt. 10).

He explains the mentoring relationship that the student is not above the teacher, just as a servant is not above the master: "It is enough for the student to be like his teacher" (Matt. 10:24).

A mentor is a trusted advisor. The basic mentoring relationship is friendship with someone who has more experience and acts as a guide to a less experienced person. This may be done in regards to a profession, job, career, or developmental stage.

A mentor functions as a teacher who enhances a person's skills and intellectual development. They act as sponsors, someone who may use his or her influence for the other's entry and advancement.

A mentor is a guide or a host, someone who welcomes and initiates another into a job or an occupation. He or she acquaints them with its values, customs, resources, and cast of characters.

Mentors are expected to set an example. They should be able to inspire a person to desire to emulate them. They should be someone another can admire. Mentors provide counsel and moral support in time of stress. They are facilitators of another's vision, dream, goal, or vocation.

The mentor also acts as a challenger in the complex relationship between mentor and mentee. The may find themselves in a position where they must push, probe, ask, and challenge, suggesting alternative ways. They may have to hug, hold, and cajole.

The mentoring process can take the form of peer counseling, formal and informal networking, support groups outside of leadership, letter-writing, and telephone calls. Mentoring can take place through casual, trusted relationships and by collecting and recollecting stories, telling them to each other.

An emerging consensus is the importance of mentoring and being mentored. Mentors play important roles in the recovery process in Alcoholic Anonymous. In business, mentors guide emerging leaders, directing them through the maze of traditional unwritten laws and rituals to positions of influence within corporations.

In many communities, it is important for adult men and women to mentor "at risk" youth or any youth "in danger" rather than endangered. In the church, the value of a class leader or prayer partner as a guide to help in the assimilation of other members is of great importance. Coaching a new convert through spiritual transformation and the nurture and support of other members has a long history of value and worth.

Ministerial alliances, ecclesiastical conferences, and special-interest groups act as role models and mentors guides to facilitate the preparation, growth, training and support of men and women called to the gospel ministry.

Mentors can be a source of critical strength, help, and support for leaders who happen to be women. They can resource a mentee early in their careers and through the years as well. Linda P in his or her young career. Mentors help you reach your major goals in life.[1]

In a mentor, look for a person who has an excellent reputation. They should have excellent credentials, be a professional, and someone you'd like to talk to. The potential mentor should have demonstrated competencies in your specific area of interest, preferably one who is ahead of you. Seek out those who have had experience guiding and assisting others. They should also be on the same track of responsibilities.

How you feel in their presence is important. If you are not comfortable in the presence of a potential mentor or their initial reaction to you is negative, reconsider your choice. Be sure they are well-informed about the career, program, group, or company you need help in.

The mentoring relationship can be both a blessing and a burden. It is a blessing because the strength of the mentor is utilized to help the mentee. The mentor is engaged in developing the next generation of leadership. They are able to pass on a wealth of experience and wisdom that go beyond formal education. They also share the secrets of the "This is how it works around here, and this is how you get things done in this organization." They can explain the nuances of climbing the leadership environment. A mentor can encourage responsible service beyond self.

The mentee experiences the security of confessing their problems with a trusted advisor and in a trusted environment. They have the joy of giving progress reports to someone who has taken an interest in them and their career. The confidence of sharing information that remains confidential. A mentee benefits from someone who will navigate them through what can be treacherous corporate waters.

Mentoring can be a burden because it is a transitional relationship, according to Daniel Levinson in *The Seasons of a Man's Life*. It can end in conflict, hurt, resentment, bitter feelings, with complex reasons for destructive termination.

Mentoring requires maturity and a strong resistance against many things, like the urge to compete with the person you are mentoring. They must have a strong resistance against being envious of another's position or jealous about their talents. The urge to clone you may be great, but please resist. One of you is enough!

It takes time to mentor—sharing compassion, maintaining confidences, discerning explicit and implicit behavior, and maintaining openness. The mentoring relationship can be a burden when the mentor is too beset by the stresses of survival to provide good mentoring.

Mentoring takes maturity. It requires wrestling with your own demons before helping someone with theirs. It takes an honest assessment of your own strengths and weaknesses, patience, and a willingness to share. It takes vulnerability to allow another person to look inside your methodologies.

The responsibility can be draining if the person being mentored sees the relationship beyond student-teacher. When someone uses mentoring as a crutch, the relationship may become obsessive. Too much dependency fosters an unhealthy mentor relationship.

The separation of mentor and mentee can be bitter. It may be that each has outgrown the other. One may be threatened by the lack of what was a professional resource between them. An example of the termination of mentoring relationships is the separation of Freud and Jung; F. Scott Fitzgerald and Hemingway; Jesus and the disciples who betrayed him with a kiss—Judas

If mentoring is to be transforming and not terminated bitterly, mentors need to know when to let go; mentees need to know when it's time to depart. Mentors must let go of expectations of who he or she is becoming without the mentor.

The need and reason for mentoring is not a sign of weakness or failure, but an opportunity for growth. It is an opportunity to affirm and encourage mentees, equipping each other for ministry and other careers contributing to building up the body of Christ.

Each of us can recall a time when we wanted someone to talk to; to know about; and help us to discover clarity on the direction in which we need to go.

Each of us can recall a time when we needed someone, in the right place and at the right time, just to call our name; or remember who we are; affirm what God has already spoken; say Amen to the work of the Holy Spirit in us to help us understand that we're not going crazy—we're just called, we are in transition; we are in the midst of transformation.

Each of us can recall a time when we wanted someone to say, "This is the way, walk in it; this is the path to take, door to open, and relation to build." Who reveals the success and a relationship with Jesus Christ in the midst of our human tragedy and brokenness? Who reveals to us that all things are possible through Jesus Christ?

Each of us can recall a time when we wanted a word fitly spoken in season—a friend, group of friends, teacher, guide—a mentor who brings out the ideals and convictions stirring within us, and as a mentor introduces us to aspects of ourselves of which we are unaware, a facilitator of spiritual growth that ultimately matures, strengthens, and compels us forward to fulfill the unique calling that is ours.

It helps if there is someone who helps us encounter our deeper self, which Carl Jung calls "the larger and greater personality maturing within us."

THE MENTORING OF MOSES

Leadership is an important subject in the word of God. If you have the gift of leadership, you are admonished to govern diligently (Rom. 12:8). Respect for discipline and authority is called for (Heb. 13:17).

God's criterion for leadership is different than humankind's. We look at external factors such as physical features, wardrobe, training, skills, and experience. God looks at the heart (1 Sam. 16:7).

Eligibility is not based on family heritage, gender, or ethnic origin: "There is no longer Jew or Greek, there is no longer slave or free, there is no longer male nor female; for all of you are one in Christ Jesus" (Gal. 3:28). God is involved with the choosing, training, dispatching, and defrocking.

Samuel was selected as a child to lead while serving in God's temple. God sent Samuel to anoint Saul as Israel's first king. God became disappointed in Saul's leadership, and Samuel was sent to anoint another, David.

Isaiah stood at ease dropping in on a heavenly conversation. He responded to the call for leadership. Sampson and John the Baptist were chosen from conception to be leaders. Esther was prepared and nurtured for leadership out of the sight of the people but in the sight of God. Deborah was chosen by God to judge Israel for forty years. Micah records that Miriam was just as much prophet as Moses and Aaron (Micah 6:4). Mary was chosen to carry the Word made flesh, and the woman at the well was reassigned to become the evangelist of Sychar, leading the people out of the city to see Jesus.

A pharaoh arose who did not know Joseph. He may or may not have been aware of Joseph's contribution towards saving Egypt from famine. This new pharaoh was not inclined to look upon Joseph's descendants with favor.

The Hebrews grew and prospered. Their increasing size may have posed a threat to the stability of Egypt. It could have been a simple ploy to maintain control, or they needed to institute a building program based on free labor, that the Hebrews became slaves. They were segregated into Gesham where they built pyramids in a land that did not recognize or acknowledge their God.

One way to control a minority community is to control its male population. The Hebrew male was a military threat and a threat by the procreation of their race. The Egyptians instituted an involuntary birth control system. The midwives were required by law to allow the daughters to live and the male babies die.

God protected Moses from genocide. An unwed foster mother raised him in sight of his birth mother in the enemy's household. He slept where the enemy slept. He read books from Pharaoh's library. He grew up among the customs and mannerisms of the Egyptian masters. He was familiar with the personalities of the protagonists. He knew their strengths and weaknesses.

Moses was an excellent candidate to dismantle Pharaoh's disenfranchisement economic program based upon a system of slave labor. He was one trained in the enemy's camp, but had a heart opened to God.

James M. Kouzes and Barry Z. Posner in *The Leadership Challenge* suggest that there are five fundamental practices of exemplary leadership.[2] These behaviors are: challenge the process, inspire a shared vision, enable others to act, model the way, and encourage the heart.

A review of the life and ministry of the prophet Moses reflects these principles. According to Kouzes and Posner, a leader is a risk-taker who ventures out into the unknown. They are innovators and experimenters to do things a better way. Moses returned to Egypt after a forty-year involuntary exile to confront Pharaoh. He challenged him with powerful, divinely conceived demonstrations to convince him it was in his best interest to let the Hebrews leave. Moses understood his own weakness. At his behest, God empowered Aaron to speak for Moses, a stutterer. Moses empowered other people. There was the prophetic gifting of seventy elders (Num. 11:24–30).

He was an example of devotion. He exemplified a relationship with God through prayer and obedience. Moses inspired the people to believe that God would deliver them from Egypt's clutches. He gave God's command about how they were to relate to God and each other. Moses had a sense of a divine call. The people had a sense that God had given him unique skills and authority. The people bought into Moses. They then bought into God's vision. Moses was an exemplary leader. Even good leaders need help every now and then. It was a leadership issue. Moses had basic management problems.

He was able to lead the people to freedom, but had a hard time getting them to the Promised Land. The problems of the wilderness appeared to be inappropriate planning rather than a failure in leadership. Moses had a location problem. He could not move the people beyond the wilderness for forty years. He had a resource problem. There was a lack of food and water. Moses had personnel problems. Doubt, fear, and low morale led to an incident with a golden calf while Moses was on Mount Sinai, seeking God. Moses had staff problems. Aaron and Miriam challenged his leadership.

Moses had a mentor. Jethro, the Midean priest, was that mentor. He was also Moses' father-in-law, Zipporah's father. He came for a visit while they were camped at the mount of God.

Moses bows down to greet him, respecting him as his elder and the head of the household. He greets him in Bedouin manner with a kiss. They retired to Moses' tent where they discussed the recent events of liberation. Moses gave a progress report about the deliverance and the desert wandering. Jethro acknowledges the power of Yahweh. A ceremonial meal was served that resembled a communion meal before God. Aaron and the other elders joined them with sacrifices and breaking of bread.

The following day, Jethro observes Moses' administration. He watched the prophet of God serve as a judge for the people. The people stood around him from morning until the evening. It was a long, exhaustive day interpreting the law and administering judgments. Jethro counseled Moses: "Listen now to me, and I will give you some advice, and may God be with you" (Exod. 18:19).

He told him that, first, what he was doing was not right. Moses was carrying too much of the leadership load. He would wear out before satisfying the people. The people would also become weary. Jethro suggested to Moses that he first teach the people the laws and decrees of God. Teach the people their duties before God and how to live.

Secondly, Jethro advised Moses to delegate his responsibilities. He should select persons who are honest and trustworthy to serve as officials over thousands, hundreds, fifties, and tens. Moses' prophetic standing could have gotten in the way of administrative advice. Jethro's intrusion was given without invitation. After all, if Moses got the people out, he could handle the trip to the Promised Land. However, many times the energy it takes to create something is different from the energy it takes to sustain it.

To his credit, Moses accepted the assistance. He received Jethro's suggestion graciously. He was comfortable enough in the mentoring relationship to receive constructive criticism without fear that Jethro did not have his best interest at heart.

He put officers over thousands, hundreds, and fifties. These officers took care of the small issues. Every great and difficult problem went to Moses. The success of giving and receiving advice may have a lot to do with Jethro's approach to mentoring. There are six steps that offer a good pattern for any mentor in the twenty-first century. Following the process does not guarantee a good mentoring, but the steps serve as a guide to enhance your own mentoring relationships.

Step One: Jethro made a personal visit. Telephone calls, letters, and e-mails provide means for the transmission of information. Reports from newspapers, magazine articles, friends, and other interested parties may provide a perspective. The information received is based upon someone else's interpretation of people and events. Nothing beats seeing things live and in living color. This gives you the opportunity to come to your own conclusions, not prejudiced by another's motives or misconceptions.

Step Two: Jethro spent time with Moses. He did not rush the visit, but set aside an appropriate amount of time to catch up on Moses' career as God's prophet. Some things take time, like good cheese and good fruitcake. Time allows the mentee to relax and disclose at levels deeper than the superficial events of the day. It allows the space to get to know another's joys and fears, dreams and heartaches, prides and prejudices. Plan for time in the visit to explore what hinders and enhances the performance of the mentee.

Step Three: He listened to Moses. Their time together was not for Jethro to tell him his business, but to listen to the progress report of Moses. It wasn't about Jethro, it was about Moses. Many leaders have no one with whom to share their good news. Others may be jealous over their success. Some may misunderstand the movement of God in their lives. Then there are those who view progress reports as bragging and grandstanding. Jethro was someone Moses could count on to appreciate his achievements.

Step Four: He affirmed Moses. Moses knew that God was doing extraordinary things through him. History was being made. A group of people went in to Egypt to escape famine in Palestine and came out a nation. He had been at the center of phenomenal miracles. He saw the Nile turn to blood, the Red Sea part, bread rain from heaven, and bitter waters turn sweet. This was no ordinary career path. Jethro was delighted to hear it. It is wonderful that others confirm what has happened in you, with you and those you influence. "Now I know that the Lord is greater than all other gods, for he did this to those who treated Israel arrogantly," said Jethro (Exod. 18:11).

Step Five: Jethro scrutinized Moses' administration before giving advice. Jethro observed Moses' method of working with the people from morning until evening. This was no quick observation. He viewed Moses long enough to make an honest assessment of what was taking place. Jethro did not interrupt Moses to respond to his techniques. He either took great notes or recorded mentally all that Moses was doing

Step Six: He gave advice. Jethro give the advice without sugar coating. He gave it without threats, warnings, or admonitions. There were no citations to research studies or allusions to what he or other leaders were doing in similar circumstances. He did not say the proverbial, "If I were you I'd. . . . " Jethro's wise counsel was twofold: teach and delegate. He didn't give too much or too little. He furnished the right amount of wisdom that gave direction to his leadership. He gave clear and concise advice.

Step Seven: He returned to his own work. Jethro did not stand over Moses while he instituted a change in his management system strategy. He gave his advice. Moses accepted it. It was up to Moses to institute the transition.

In this way, Moses is not too dependent upon Jethro. The father-in-law gives Moses space to learn to work out the solution his own way. He did not do it for him. He did not hold his hand through it. He did not announce to the people, for Moses, the problem or the solution.

Jethro gave the advice and went to take care of his own business. If Moses needed further guidance, he could contact him. Jethro knew enough not to smother Moses with the mentor relationship.

Leaders need help sometimes. There are several ways to help leaders. Mentoring is one way to help. Another way is demonstrated in the following sermon. Moses employs a spiritual weapon to assist Joshua on the battlefield.

THE WORD

Whenever Moses held up his hand, Israel prevailed; and whenever he lowered his hand, Amalek prevailed.—Exodus 17:11

I Got Your Back

Everyone needs help sometimes. In the lull of the daily minutia or in the heat of the battle, we may need help. The cause may be correct, but we still need help. The resources may be plentiful, but we still need help. The staff may be expertly trained, but we still need help. The leadership may have an excellent track record of achievement, but we still need help. Morale may be high, but we still need help.

Moses demonstrated a method of offering help when it was needed. He provided the kind of help that went beyond the help he provided as an emancipator of Israel from the clutches of Egypt. It extended beyond the courage to confront Pharaoh; the daring to risk his own life; the boldness to walk into the enemy's camp; the chutzpah to talk back to a ruler who believed he had absolute power.

Moses' help went beyond intestinal fortitude to negotiate Israel's doubts and Egypt's arrogance. He gave up his personal agenda, but he did more. He took up God's agenda and still did more.

The kind of help Moses provided Israel is shown in the pericope, Exodus 17:6–16. Moses helped by being an intercessor. Intercession is a way of helping people. It moves you from what you want to what they need. It shifts the center of gravity from you to them. The needs of others replace your own needs and concerns.

Richard Foster writes that people are desperate for the help that intercessory prayer can provide. Families are being torn apart and people are living desperate lives without hope, future, or purpose. The people of God can make a difference in the lives of people by becoming intercessors. We need to learn how to pray on their behalf.

Moses was an excellent example of a leader who knows the power of intercessory prayer. Every time Israel needed help, Moses prayed on their behalf. When Pharaoh wouldn't let them out, Moses prayed until the day of deliverance. When the desert was hot, the sun was scorching, and the trip from Africa became long, the people tired and thirsty, Moses helped again.

The people turned against Moses and against God. Moses interceded. "What shall I do with your people?"—God answered with water. When the water was bitter, Moses interceded. God made the bitter waters sweet. The people were hungry. Moses interceded and manna daily fell from heaven. When they got tired of heavenly bread, Moses prayed again and they were given quail to eat.

Israel was about to face her first military confrontation. They met the Amalekites at a place called Rephidim. It means in Hebrew "resting place." Rephidim meant one thing, but would mean another to the Israelites. The place that means relief, rest, and refreshment is now the place where they would engage the enemy. Instead of a resting place, Rephidim became a battlefield.

Have you ever found that your resting place was the place where the enemy was waiting for you? You expected a relief station and found a battleground instead. What you were looking for, wanted, and needed has now been turned into a war zone.

Moses' way of helping was twofold. Joshua would lead the army into the valley to fight. Moses would go to the mountain with two lieutenants, Aaron and Hur, to pray. While Joshua was engaged in physical warfare, Moses was engaged in spiritual warfare. Joshua fought with sword and shield, while Moses fought with prayer and perseverance.

Moses had the hardest task. He stretched out his arms and became the intercessor between Yahweh and the people. Moses arms grew tired. He lowered them. When he stopped interceding, he saw that the enemy began to gain.

Moses again lifted his arms and prayed. The battle began to go in their favor. Aaron and Hur had to step in to help Moses. They put a rock under the prophet so that he could sit down. They helped him by holding his arms up in place while he continued to seek God.

Moses was the intercessory who inspired the people in battle. What I like about Aaron and Hur is that they saw what needed to be done and did it. They remained close enough to the task to be available. They were ready to assist leadership. They perhaps understood that it was a "we thing," not a "me thing."

Aaron and Hur were not only available but were willing to go the distance. They were willing to stay as long as it was necessary to get the job done. They were willing to work to task, not to time.

In the end, it would be Joshua who would get most of the credit for the battle, not Moses. The one out front gets the credit. Usually the one in the midst of the conflict gets a pat on the back and a thank you.

Behind the battle, backing up the battle, was the battle of intercession. Joshua engaged the enemy on the physical battlefield and Moses engaged the enemy in the spiritual realm. Joshua was not left alone in battle because Moses was interceding, backing him up in prayer. Moses in essence was saying, "I got your back"! That's what we need to do for each other. I got your back with prayer.

P. T. Forsyth suggests that the greater the pressure, the greater the need for intercessory prayer. He says the deeper one plunges into the valley of decision, the higher one must rise on the mountain prayer. We must hold up the hands of those whose major responsibility is to prevail with God.

The more you go, the more you do; the higher you fly, the more you need someone interceding for you. The greater the risk, the harder the task, the more you need someone backing you up in prayer. The more you fight your way out of the wilderness and into God's promised places, the more you need someone backing you up in prayer.

Everybody needs backup. The children who are born addicts, who begin to breathe and go through crack withdrawal at the same time, need back up. The families who are evicted, the homeless digging through garbage looking for food, and the elderly who cannot afford their medication need back up. Children taking their first smoke on a cigarette or marijuana need backup. Newlyweds, young parents, and those who have not made a commitment to a life partner need backup.

Every leader needs backup. Those who are breaking new ground need backup. The risk takers in every field need backup. The leaders trying to establish new paradigms need backup. Scientists are wrestling with the ethical questions of cloning a human. They need backup. Laboratory scientists who are creating new diseases and drugs need backup. Champions of justice, judges, attorneys, juries, and lawmakers need backup.

The more hurt we see, despair we experience, and the more hell we see on earth, somebody needs to be praying! We need backup. There is a song that expresses the same sentiment: "Somebody prayed for me, had me on their mind."

Let me tell you what importance Moses' intercessory prayer had on Israel that day. Foster indicates that intercessory prayer can be described as "wrestling." Harry Emerson Fosdick describes prayer as a battleground.

Moses was wrestling on a spiritual battleground. He struggled in a real conflict on a spiritual battlefield so that Israel could engage the enemy properly. An enemy will continue to be a danger unless we confront them. Confrontation gives you an opportunity to win. Backup prayer gave them the courage to discover the depth of their faith in God. It gave them confidence in God and in themselves in the face of the enemy. It is one thing to say how good, strong, and mighty you are at home, it's another thing to say it in front of those who want to wipe you off the face of the earth.

Moses, the intercessor, inspired them to endure the day's ups and downs, backs and forths, sometimes winning and sometimes losing. Many soldiers die in battle. Not because they cannot fight, but because they cannot handle the uncertainty of the battle.

Some people cannot take the "in-between" nature of conflicts and challenges. They cannot take the in-between thing—in between jobs, relationships, life styles, efforts, the almost, the not yet, or the soon to be. Intercessory prayer gives them the power to keep fighting, even through the indecision of the day.

The power of intercessory prayer helped them endure the temptation to quit. When the battle starts to go the other way, it is easy to quit, move, get out, jump ship, leave, or surrender. Prayer prevailed on the mountain so that the people could prevail in the valley.

Joshua's firepower was backed up with Moses' prayer power. You just may be able to get a little more, go a little further, do a little more, jump a little higher, when you are backed up with prayer power. The army was able to fight as long as Moses was praying. He prevailed in prayer, and the enemy was defeated.

· Our battles are fought and won on our knees. We need to wrestle on spiritual battlefields to back up our family, church, community, and leadership. Intercessory prayer is the battlefield where the faithful must endure. It is the place where temptations are dealt with, where we engage the evil and fight distractions that divert us from God's way.

Who backs up the intercessor? The Lord is your back up. Jesus, a priest after the order of Melchizedek, is always making intercession for us (Heb. 7:25). "It is Christ Jesus, who died, yes, who was raised, who is at the right hand of God, who indeed intercedes for us " (Rom. 8:34); "There is only one mediator between God and humankind, Jesus Christ" (1 Tim. 2:5).

Jesus got your back! He grants us access into heaven's throne room. Jesus fixes our prayers before they get to God. He straightens them out and cleans them up. Holy God. The Lord's prayers sustain our desire to pray. Jesus is our Aaron. Aaron and Hur were there to help Moses. Jesus is here for us, our eternal intercessor. And as a result, we are enabled to pray for others with a new authority. Everybody needs help. Every leader needs help. Let us pray as a first thing and not as a thing of last resort.

Intercessory prayer is a backup strategy that works. You will find that as you intercede for others, God will be working on your issues. You will be strengthened in prayer. Your faith will increase as you pray with results.

Look someone in the eye and assure them today by saying, I got your back! It may make all the difference in the world.

Chapter seven

Taking Care of Business

༄

O NE OF THE LESSONS we are taught early in life from the dinner table, on the baseball diamond, tennis court, on the gridiron, shooting marbles, playing tea, house, dolls; is to play fair. In our formative years, it seems that the greatest effort was placed on our learning to play fair. To assure that everyone got the lessons straight, coaches taught us not only to win the game, but also to play fair. We should shake the hand of the opponent following the game, whether you win, lose, or draw.

Leaving nothing to human nature, there were referees. They were the ones who enforced the rules of the game, oversaw the process, and guaranteed as much as possible that the playing field remained even. Penalties were levied upon those who would take undue and unfair advantage during the game, such as roughing the kicker, pass interference, zone defense, or clipping. That was an admission to the reality that there would be those who would not play fair.

Then there are the onlookers whose presence applied the necessary pressure on participants that the game would be played fair. These were the people who sat on their front porch while you played stickball in the streets. They were the ones standing around the fringes of basketball cages in urban anywhere America. They are the people in the stands, who without instant replay or play-by-play announcers, kept the referees honest so that the game would be played fair.

We are just as concerned about playing fair today as we were in our sandlot days. Many ascribe to what I call "Faironomics." Faironomics is the presence of fairness in financial matters. Faironomics is the thought that says those who want to work, should work, because that's fair.

People who work should earn fair wages, that's fair. Those who work should have the same fair chance at promotions and raises, that's fair. The qualifications for employment should not include gender, race, ethnic origin, or religious preferences, because that's fair. You get what you pay for, that's fair.

Faironomics says that everyone should be able to participate in the flow of goods and services, producing as well as consuming, that's fair. Everyone should have the opportunity to support themselves and their families in the environment of their choice, that's fair. Everyone can live wherever they can afford to live and the only color necessary to sign a lease, a mortgage, to purchase a home or land, rent an apartment, or buy an automobile is green, because that's fair. Everyone should have equal access to the tools for economic survival so they can participate and contribute to the economy, that's fair.

"Fairism" is the influence of fair in governing affairs. Fairism is the thought that whatever community you and I live in, you should have a say in. There is no taxation without representation, except in the District of Columbia. There is one vote per voice; you may vote your choice, that's fair.

Once elected, you can hold those persons accountable for the services they render, that's fair. Fairism says that fair elections are held at regular intervals, and he or she who has the most votes, wins. You can speak your mind, say what you will, even if others oppose it; you may write your thoughts without fear of retribution; you can object, joining yourself with like-minded individuals in civil disobedience, that's fair.

Fairism, the influence of fair, says that the educational system provides for each child because every child should have a chance to learn, because every child can learn, that's fair. Fairism says that you are guilty until you are proven innocent—I mean innocent until proven guilty, that's fair. You have a right to a trial by the press—I mean you have a right to a trial by your peers. You have a right to a fair hanging—I mean, you have a right to a fair hearing. You have a right to drive responsibly, following the rules of the road, except when you are driving while black.

One group does not have the right to more or less than any other group, whether it is in economics, housing, or education. The playing field is still tilted, and fairism says adjustments need to be made in the court house, school house, both house of Congress, banking house, brokerage house, sporting house, and your momma's house.

When you are "fairconscious," you are raising the level of awareness about fair in every aspect of your life. That means that you would not dare do for one of your children without doing for the others. One child is not favored above the others, as best you can. If you have five children and one piece of candy, the candy will be divided five ways, that's fair. If there is only enough soup for one, water would be added so that all five would be able to eat, that's fair.

Fairconsciousness says that you create an environment so that there is equal access, equal opportunity, fair shakes, and fair deals for everyone within your influence. It is being conscious of fair on a personal level.

You make sure that fair challenges evil and unjust systems wherever they are, even in the land of the free and the home of the brave. Fair exposes racist, classist, prejudicial actions and activities, overt and convert, that's fair.

Fairconsciousness is intolerant of exclusionary tactics, clauses, and causes. Fair has had a hard time with unfair. In fact, nonviolence has always had a rough time with violence, good with evil, chaos with organization, excellence with mediocrity, construction with destruction, justice with oppression, and oil with water . . . it just does not mix.

A "fair theology" speaks the fair-mindedness of God. It is the God-knowledge of fair. God shows no partiality; the sun shines on the just and the unjust; God saves through Christ everyone who calls upon His name.

In Christ, all persons are accepted. There is neither Jew nor Gentile, male or female. We are all one in Christ Jesus. That is fair theology—God knowledge of fair.

The cross is God's major statement on fair. All sins are nailed to His cross, white sins, black sins, Hispanic sins. To the cross was nailed urban sins, rural sins, high and mighty, low-down-and-dirty messy sins, social sins, pew sins, pulpit sins, and glory to God, your sins and my sins.

The fair theology of God means that the resurrection was for everyone. No one country, city, county, nation, or group of people owns or controls the result of the resurrection. God fixed it so that when Jesus rose early that Sunday morning, he shook death off, overcame evil, set Satan straight, fooled the living hell out of hell, defied rigormortis, and got up, not for some, but for everyone. That's fair!

But we have lived long enough to know that people don't play fair. In economics, education, housing, social, and civic affairs, whatever, people don't play fair. That is why God sends a few coaches to teach us again about what's fair. The Holy Spirit becomes the referee, convicting and confronting.

When a pharaoh arose who did not know Joseph and the Hebrews were segregated to the mud pits of Goshen to make brick without straw, God called coach Moses to go over and coach Pharaoh into a fair consciousness. Tell him to let my people go.

When Hamon unfairly tried to promote his legislation, coach Esther was called into action. When the Babylonian judgment, in the fullness of time, ended, God sent Nehemiah to usher in the fair-mindedness of God. Nehemiah was charged with the task of community-building, and his neighbors were not being fair.

When Sistera ravaged Israel, God raised up a coach be the name of Deborah. When Goliath was selling wolf tickets in the valley, God sent for a rookie coach from the taxi-squad to teach Goliath about fair play.

When sin dominated humankind and stood between God and His creation, the Lamb of God left heaven to save his people from their sins. When apartheid become another artificial human category to disenfranchise a people from their voice, their say, their land, dreams, country, God sent coach Mandela to storm the gates of oppression and usher in the fair mindedness of God.

When segregated did not mean separate but equal, and Africans in America were denied inherent unattainable rights of life, liberty and the pursuit of happiness God sent another coach, Martin Luther King Jr., a prophet whose vision of a beloved community transcended civil rights to bring the fair-mindedness of God with national and international implications. The following sermons show two of God's coaches taking care of business. The first leader is Esther, the wife of King Xerxes, who served during the second captivity of Israel in Babylon. The other is the Queen of Sheba, one of the Candace monarchs in the Meroic period in Africa.

One is a queen consort and the other a queen in her own right and authority. One is not expected to be concerned with the affairs of state. The other is the center of the affairs of state in her vast country.

One came to power by heritage, the other married into the royal family. One eagerly took the reigns of power, the other was thrust into it.

Esther reluctantly took matters into her own hands to resolve a matter that could have ended in the annihilation of her people. The Queen of Sheba came to see King Solomon perhaps over a perceived threat to her territory in the Red Sea.

Esther used a non-direct approach to work her issue. The Queen of Sheba used the direct approach. Esther employed her spiritual disciplines and the other used politics.

Each of these women contributes to the understanding of leadership. There is no one-way to do it. Everyone can learn leader behaviors and principles. It is best not to imitate leader traits and methods exactly. Incorporate them into your repertoire to the uniqueness of your personality and position.

THE WORD

Go, gather all the Jews to be found in Susa, and hold a fast on my behalf, and neither eat nor drink for three days, night or day. I and my maids will also fast as you do. After that I will go to the king, though it is against the law; and if I perish, I perish.—Esther 4:16

Armed and Dangerous

When was the moment that you realized that you were a grown woman? I mean when was the moment, the minute, the hour, the second, the month, the year? When was the moment that you realized you were grown? When did you know you were a big girl now? When did you know there was to be no more foolishness? You are big enough to pay your own bills. You are grown enough now to clean up your own messes, live on your own, and live by yourself.

You are grown now—no longer wooed by passing fancies because you are grown. You are grown—grown to know your own style; grown so that you know what you want.

You are grown enough to think complex concepts and think deep thoughts. You have at least an idea of where you are going from this moment.

You are grown, and you are able to make up your own mind. Everybody else is shaving his or her head, but you know that a shaved head is not you. Spandex looks good on somebody, but you know it is not for you. Braids are not for everybody. Weaves are not for everybody. Wigs are not for everybody. Cornrows are not for everybody. You are grown and you know what is for you and what is not for you.

You are no longer confused about direction; you have uncovered some sense of purpose. You can be determined about some things. You can be directed and you know that you are not yet perfect. You are just grown.

You can rule your own house because you are grown. You can make your own bed because you are grown. You can fix your own food, or are at least on speaking terms with Sarah Lee and Betty Crocker. You are grown.

You can make reasonable decisions. You can face the music. You can pay the piper for the dance you have been dancing. You can lie in the bed that you made for yourself now because you are grown. You're a grown woman, no longer wondering what life is all about. You're living it.

You are grown, girl. You put away childish things. You have grown beyond the center of the universe. You have grown beyond "it is mine" and "I have to have it" and "I have to have it now." You are not blaming other people for your problems anymore. You are grown.

You have grown beyond the high school stuff: "You can only be my friend. You can't be her friend. If you are going to be my friend, then you can't be her friend."

When was the moment you realized you were grown? Grown means you know your own mind and you know your own body. When you are a grown woman, you have already figured out what you have and what it is going to be. You are what you are and there is no point getting upset and angry. Don't worry about other women's figures. If they have more curves than you do, don't worry about it. If they are slimmer than you, don't worry about it.

When you are grown, no matter what you have, you know how to handle it. You know how to work with what you have. You know how to present what you have. You are grown, and you know you can work with it! If you are really grown, no one will really know for sure whether your curves are real or fake.

You are grown now and your mother is no longer your enemy. In fact, you are so grown now that you realize that she was right all along. In fact, on a good day, you will confess that you are beginning to sound a lot like her and you are beginning to look a lot like her. But that's all right because you are grown.

When you are grown, you can take care of your own dirty stuff. You can take care of your own dirty dishes and you can handle your own dirty linen. You know how to clean up after yourself. You don't let all your dirty stuff hang out so that others can see how dirty it has gotten.

You are grown now, you can keep your stuff straight and you can manage your money. You are grateful that you have some money to manage. You are grown now and you can budget a little. You can sacrifice. You can engage in some delayed gratification. That means you can wait for stuff because you are grown now. You know that you don't have to have it right now. You can just put it on layaway. You don't have to have it right now. You can stop and wait for your turn to come.

You are grown now and you can seek counsel because you know that you don't know everything. You are grown and can analyze a little bit. You can rationalize a little bit.

You are grown now and you can think through stuff. You just don't do things impulsively. You can handle your responsibilities and you can endure moments of weakness.

You have survived disappointment. You have collected enough regrets, like signatures in your high school yearbook; but you are grown now. You have lived long enough to know that you can make it.

Being grown goes beyond combing your hair and tying your own shoes. It goes beyond making your own choices and suffering the consequences for the wrong ones. Being grown is more than crossing the street and looking both ways. It is more than a point on your personal time line.

Being grown is not just determined by a chronological passage of time. There are women who have lived a long time and still are not grown. There are women who have crossed beyond their thirties and their forties and their fifties and still are not grown.

They may have navigated start-up scenarios, but are not grown. They still have not cut the umbilical cord. They are still dependent and have not learned how to be independent. Every crisis is the one that is going to knock them out of the box. But grown women have survived enough traumas on their own to believe that they can get up and start all over again. Are you a member of the grown women's club?

God gives us the privilege to take a look at one of God's own grown women in action. Her story is found in the book of Esther.

This book is one of those rare pieces of divine narratives in which the name of God is not mentioned. But the presence of God is inferred.

Many times the Bible does not include much data about the women contained within the sixty-six books. Often they are relegated to the margins and to the footnotes of the events of God's people. Personal history is excluded and they are often identified by everything other than their names. They are identified by location, like the women of Tekoa or the woman at the well. Sometimes, they are identified by relationships, like the mother of James or Peter's mother-in-law. Sometimes, they are identified by circumstances, like the woman with the issue of blood or the woman caught in adultery. Many are simply identified as the "woman." Nobody remembers their names. They are just remembered by their situation. We don't want to be identified by our problems. We don't want to be just identified just by our circumstances. Nobody knows your name, nobody understands your personal identity, but your public problem simply becomes the identity of your life. It is no longer who you are because it gets lost in what you are doing.

In this case, the woman has a name. Her historical data is included, her personal information is disclosed. She is the undisputed heroine at what could have been a tragic event in the lives of the Jews. Hadassah is her Hebrew name. Esther is her Babylonian name. The name Esther was given to Hadassah by her captives and by her oppressors. Throughout the book, we find the story of Esther. In other words, those in charge of her named her. If you allow somebody to name you, they often assume the privilege of controlling you.

Now some nicknames are nice and some nicknames are not nice. If somebody decides to call you out of your name and it is negative, it is offensive. It is the opposite of who God says that you are. Don't allow that person the power to name you or control you. You correct them: No, I am not Stinky. I am not Boo-Boo. No, I am not Big Feet. No, I am not Crazy. This is my name and I will not allow you to change my identity and control who I am."

There are grown folks known their whole lives as "Bump." They even call themselves Bump. No one really ever knows his or her names. They are only known only as Bump. Bump is the Chief Executive Officer and President of a major corporation. Bump's identity is trapped in a nickname.

The book of Esther begins with Vashti who was the queen. She defied Ahasuerus, the king. He had given a direct order to present herself before his drunken court after a hundred and twenty days of celebration. Because she refused to present herself, the king's advisers told him that she needed to be banished because the other women of the community would feel that they had a right to refuse their husbands' requests. And so she was banished from the kingdom.

When the king sobered up, his world looked a little bit different. How many of you understand what I just said? When you come to yourself, you are no longer under the influence of other substances., all of a sudden, the world looks a little bit different.

While he was under the influence, the world looked one way; but as soon as he became sober, reality started to sink in. When reality stared him in the face, he suddenly realized that the woman he loved and cared about was gone. She had been banished from his sight and from his kingdom.

His advisors tried to help him deal with his new reality. They suggested that he get a new queen. In Esther 2:8, many girls were taken to the palace in Susa and put in the care of Hegai. There, Hadassah was chosen and pampered. She had hair treatments and foot treatments. There were spices to anoint her body so that her skin would be smooth and silky. She had the best hairdresser at her command. She was able to select from an extensive wardrobe those things that were just her color and would fit her style. In other words, girlfriend was a kept woman.

Let's be real: we have to be careful about those personalities who like kept women. I am not talking a foreign language here. It is nice to be wanted and every woman wants to be wanted.

Women want to be able to see their reflections in masculine eyes. Women want men to appreciate who they are and what they are about. Women want a man to stand in their corner—a man to applaud their performances and somebody to appreciate them. It is not that other women can't appreciate us, but it is something about having men appreciate us that makes a difference.

Every woman wants to be wanted. But there is a difference between being wanted and being possessed. You may not want to be part of a harem. You may not want to be a call girl. You may not want to be kept waiting for him to come around. You may not want the pager he's given you so he can locate you any day and any time of the week. He keeps tabs on you and notices how long it takes you to call him after he pages. Baby, that's not being wanted; that's being kept!

You can't go anywhere unless you ask permission to go. You can't see anybody unless you ask permission to be seen. You can't be friends with anybody unless you ask permission to be friends. You can't buy anything with your own money unless you ask permission. Baby, that's not being wanted; that's being kept!

Too often, we confuse the two. We say: "He just wants to hear my voice. See, the cell phone he gave me is because he loves me. See, the car he gave me is because he wants me to ride around looking good. See, the outfit that he gave me is because he knows I like this color. See, the apartment he helped me to get, it's because he wants me to live well."

No, that's not being wanted; that's being kept. That is being kept because everything you receive comes with a price tag. Just know that if he hasn't asked for it yet, he is going to ask for it later: "This is my apartment, these are my clothes, that is my pager, and that is my cell phone; and you mean to tell me that you are not going to do what I want you to do? I took you to dinner and spent all this money on you and you mean to tell me that I can't come up later on?"

My mama was a wise woman. She said not to put on anybody else's stuff to go out because you might go out there being cute and come home a cute little naked bunny when he asks for his stuff back. That's not being wanted; that is being kept. There is a difference between being wanted and being possessed and being obsessed.

Back to the text, the Word tells us that Hadassah, Esther, hid her religion, her nationality, and family background in order to be a kept woman. In order to gain the favor of a man, she had to become who she was not. She had to become somebody else. She had to assume another persona; she could not risk being exactly who she was.

My sisters, in case somebody hasn't told you, there is only so much pretending you can do. The day will come when the real you will come shining through. To help the adjustment period, you just go out today and start being real. Tell folks who you are. Tell them where you came from. Tell them where you live. Tell them what you do and where you are going. If they can't handle that, they will go on out of your life.

Isn't better that they go early rather than later after you have invested in the relationship? Once you have invested time and energy and emotion in a relationship, you are all hung up on somebody who thinks he is in love and he doesn't even know who you are.

The Word says that Hadassah passed the initiation period. She spent twelve months as a kept woman. There was a need to be sure that any offspring of the relationship would truly be the king's child. So a woman had to be kept long enough to be clear that she was a virgin when she came into the harem. Hadassah kept it simple and presented herself simply to the king and he kept asking for her by name. The Word says that he liked her above all others. He put a crown on her head and proclaimed her his queen. He held a banquet and celebration in her honor and gifts were given with royal liberality.

Time passes and scholars surmise it is now five years in the future. In those ensuing years, Haman rose in palace politics. The king favored Haman and the king gave him a seat higher than all the other nobles in the land. All of the royal officials bowed down to Haman. Haman enjoyed the power of his position and everybody in the kingdom gave Haman deference. Everybody, that is, except Mordecai.

If you want to rankle someone in power, ignore his or her position. Mordecai ignored Haman's power and position, and that made Haman angry. Can't you hear Haman: "How dare you to not recognize who I am."

Have you ever met folks like that? They have an attitude: "Don't you know who I am? Don't you understand my position in this company? Don't you know who I am in this family? Everybody is scared of me but you. What is the matter with you?"

Two of the king's eunuchs devised a plot to kill him, and Mordecai found out what had happened. He had Esther tell the king on his behalf and so the king's life was spared. Later, Haman devised a plot and told the king that it was not in his best interest to tolerate the Jews scattered throughout his kingdom. He decided that Ahasuerus had to get rid of the Jews.

Haman volunteered his own money to help eradicate the problem. He wanted a decree that all of the Jews be destroyed, young and old, women and children on a single day. The king signed it.

Mordecai learned of the plot, tore his clothes, cried, and sat in the gate with sackcloth and ashes as a sign of mourning. Esther heard and sent her eunuch to find out what the problem was. He came back with the news that the Jews were to be killed. Mordecai wanted Esther to go to the king and beg for mercy and plead for her people.

Esther's response was filled with fear: "You don't understand. I am the queen now. I have a palace. I never had a palace before. I have maids in waiting. You know, I am up here now and the living is good. I have too much to sacrifice now. I am queen.

When I was just your niece, I was just a peasant girl. I could do the stuff that you wanted, but now, I have position and power. If I jeopardize that, I might not be queen anymore. After all, we know what he did with the last queen who didn't go along with his plan and his program."

Mordecai had to explain it to her in the language that she could understand: "Don't get cute with me. Just because you are up there in the palace and you are queen and everything and you have a crown on your head, you are just a Jew like everybody else. When everybody else dies, you are going to die, too. If you don't help the cause, God will find somebody else because God has more than one person to work with. You are not the only one. God will choose somebody else. But you and your father's house will perish and be destroyed."

Having time to think about his words, Esther makes a decision to gather the people and to hold a national fast and a national prayer meeting. Esther made up her mind and decided that she would go to the king for the cause of her people. What does all of this have to do with leadership and grown women? Glad you asked. I know you are wondering.

The first thing is: Grown women own up to their past—their family history, their background, their heritage, and their religion. Grown women come clean! Grown women wake up in the morning and say they are not fronting any more. No more pretending. Grown women find the courage to come out of hiding and to stop living lies. Grown women realize that the past cannot be changed, eradicated, or erased. It matters not where you begin, but it is where you end that counts.

Moses started out in a basket on the river and ended up the prince of all Egypt, a deliverer and a liberator. Joseph started out in prison and ended up in charge of the pharaoh's palace. David started out as a shepherd boy and ended up king. Jesus started out in a manger and ended up at the right hand of God.

Grown leader women do not let the past exempt them. They do not let the past exclude them. Being grown is understanding we cannot change what is. We just have to deal with what we have. It is not where we start out, it is not where we came from, it is not who our mama is or who our daddy is, or even if we even know who mama or daddy are, but it is what you make of your life that counts. It is what you do with your adult self that matters.

Grown women are not afraid of "used to be." Didn't you used to be poor? Didn't you used to fool around? Didn't you used to be a kept woman? Didn't you used to snort cocaine? Didn't you used to shoot up heroin? Didn't you used to hang out in the bar on the corner? Didn't you used to be this and used to do that? Grown women know experiences shape us. They are able to stand up and say: "Yes, I used to, but I don't now." It does not matter what you used to be.

What we are really afraid of is "never be." We get so hung up on "used to be." No, it's "never be" that you ought to be afraid of: never be debt free; never be healed; never have enough money in the bank; never be delivered. It is the "never" thing that you ought to be praying on and praying against, not the "used to be."

You need to say: "I used to lie. I used to cheat. I used to get drunk. I used to sleep around. Yes, I used to do a whole lot of things, but look at me now, baby! I am not that any more since Jesus came into my life. I am grown now and used to be doesn't bother me anymore. I am grown now, I can own up to what I was because I am not any longer." Grown women face the past and own up to who they really are. Grown women use the past to make them strong, not bring them down.

Grown women do what they have to do at the time that it needs to be done. Grown women are responsible. Immature women are easily intimidated. As soon as a problem comes around, they say: "Let's step back. Let's unplug. We aren't going to see the king. You had better find somebody else to be that stupid."

Immature women are impatient. They are insecure—every blip on the radar screen is a cause to get depressed and go home, close the doors, and go to bed for a week. Immature women are disturbed by any kind of crisis or challenge that rises up. But grown women get over it.

Grown women say: "I don't have the answer, but I am going to try it anyhow. I am not sure where I am going, but I am certainly not going to stay here. Well, you know I may not have all the support that I need, but I am pressing my way. I may not be able to see clearly around this problem, but I am going to make my way anyhow. Yes, I have been hurt in the past, but this time it's going to be different."

Grown women make decisions based on faith and not fear. Immature women make decisions based on fear: "I am afraid my marriage is not going to work out. I am afraid my money is not going to hold out. I am afraid that the job is going to go away. I am afraid that my family is going to fall apart. I am afraid that they are going to quit on me."

Immature women are afraid of this and afraid of that, but grown women don't make decisions based on their fears. Grown women make decisions based on faith: By faith, I believe that God is able. By faith, if I perish, I perish! I believe that God can."

Grown women have moved beyond "I." They have moved beyond the singular "I," and "me," and "what I want."

Grown women have moved on to the "we" and to "us." In other words, immature women are still consumed with themselves; but grown women are able to extend their care and compassion to others. Immature women sing the song of I, but grown women sing the sing of we. Grown women risk title, they risk position, they risk name, and they risk reputation for a cause greater than themselves. Grown women understand that it is not good to rise all by themselves. When they rise all by themselves, they are targets for everybody who want to come after them. If they rise with some help, that means when the enemy comes after them, he has to go after everybody else, too. You are not a singular target; grown women know how to take folks with them. They take others with them to claim God's blessings and opportunities.

Lastly, Esther was grown. What did this grown leader woman do? What can be applied to your own leadership?

What she looked like got her an invitation to see the king. Her character got her the crown, but "whose" she was saved her people. Do you see the progression? What she looked like got her an invitation. Her character got her the crown, but it was as the daughter of God that her people were saved.

Grown women do not base their lives on the external factors of life. It is more than what you look like. It is more than the assets that God created you with. It is more than what you can put on to accentuate the assets.

It is your character that will secure the crown. It will be your character that will get you promoted. It will be your character that will get you elected to public office. It will be your character that will help keep your family together. It will be your character that someone will fall in love with and want to be with.

The external factor is just a passing fancy. There are women old enough to tell you: "Girls, it will be tight, right, high, and in its proper place when you are in your twenties, but get down around fifty and sixty! What is up is now down and what is in is now out!" Newer models and newer additions do not disturb grown women.

Brothers get caught up in newer models and new additions. You have to be grown up enough to say: "Okay, fine. You are going for younger. She cannot do better than me. Experience counts for something."

Well, what has all this have to say to grown women? Stop reaching for your horoscope; it is not going to help. Stop calling the 900 psychic lines; they are not going to help. Stop counting on your checkbook; it is not going to help. No, instead, pull out your prayers. Pull out your fasting, get your praise on, get your worship life together and then like Hadassah, you will be armed and considered dangerous. Demons will start to run. The devil will be put on notice. Hell will start to get scared. Why? Because there are some grown women are in the house and they know how to go to war. They know how to battle. They know how to connect with God and God will give them the victory. How do I know this? Because God says the battle is not yours. The battle belongs to God.

Hadassah made a decision to put God on the battlefield. She used her spiritual weapons and invited others to join her. How did she call up God? She called in prayer. How did she get the power? She fasted for the power. When the dust settled, Haman was hung on his own gallows, the gallows that he erected to hang Mordecai. His own weapon defeated the enemy. Nobody can do that but God.

Again, I ask, when was the moment that you knew you were grown? When did you know to pull out the right weapon to use to do what needed to be done at the time that it needed to be done? People in this world will tell you not to be so smart because men won't like you. They will tell you not to be so cute because women won't like you. The voices in this culture will tell you not to be so different because the world will not have a place for you. But when you are armed and considered dangerous, then you are grown up enough to say: "That's their problem. That's not my problem. Frankly, I don't care. Because I am grown, armed with spiritual weapons, and am considered dangerous."

There are two things we need to do: one, we need to issue a call for women to come into their maturity. It is not about getting old. It's about being mature. I have met some nineteen year olds that are more mature than some forty-year-old women because they are willing to step into their maturity. They were willing to pick up their spiritual weapons and use them first before meeting a crisis or challenge at hand. Before you open your mouth, ask God what to say. You may want to hit someone. But before you allow the passion and the energy to get you to do something that you will regret later on, ask God how to respond. Sometimes a crisis will make you go stark raving mad; but before you do, ask God what it is that God wants you to do now.

Pull out your spiritual weapons: pray and fast. In the midst of it all, God will give you instructions. Sometimes we have the luxury of a three-day fast and a three-day prayer like Esther. Sometimes we have to do it in three seconds. But when you are in the heat of the battle, either one can be just as effective. If you are willing to step into your maturity in Jesus Christ, then it is time to come to the altar.

The second thing we need to do is to understand that the difference between success and failure was Hadassah's relationship with God. What kept her alive was her relationship with God. Who provided the power to defeat the enemies of her people? It was her God. What were the weapons that she reached for first? It was her spiritual weapons, because the weapons of our war are not carnal but are spiritual.

The problem with us is that we haven't learned how to fight with our spiritual weapons. Now, we know how to fight. Many of us have been raised in the "hood." We know how to take care of ourselves. You know how to fight physically. You don't know how to fight spiritually and you are getting whomped.

God wants us to be able to fight spiritually with our spiritual weapons: praise, fasting, and worship. I tell you the Word of God will do more to your enemy than you can imagine, but first you have to be willing to use it. First you have to have a relationship with Christ. Are you grown? Are you tired of being a babe in

Jesus Christ? It is time to be armed and considered dangerous. The time is now.

An inexperienced immature soldier will reach for whatever weapon and resource are at hand; but grown women know how to check in with God before they go to battle. Girlfriend was a grown woman and she said: "Before I step out in space, before I endanger my life, before I endanger my wealth and reputation, before I put myself in jeopardy, I am going to reach for my spiritual weapon. Mordecai, you call everybody to pray. My household and I will pray and fast for three days. We are going to talk to God. God is going to give us a plan. God is going to let us in on the secret. God is going to show us the way. God is going to get our enemies ready for defeat."

God was going to do it because she chose the right weapon. She chose the right weapon to match the war she was in. Immature women are not sure what weapon to pull when they are in the battle. They will pull a sword when they really need a shield or they will call out the troops when they really need somebody to negotiate a treaty. But when you are grown, you are armed and considered dangerous. Before you walk out on the battlefield, you are going to consult with the General of generals. You are going to consult with the One in charge and ask God how we are going to work it out. How are we going to do this? How is this going to happen? Guess what? God gave her the plan. All she had to do was walk in the direction of the plan. God gave the enemy a defeat and the Jews and Hadassah were victorious. And God will do the same for us—if we are truly grown! If we are truly grown, we are armed and considered dangerous—for God will give us the victory!

THE WORD

When the queen of Sheba heard of the fame of Solomon, (fame due to the name of [Yahweh]), she came to test him with hard questions. She came to Jerusalem with a very great retinue, with camels bearing spices, and very much gold, and precious stones; and when she came to Solomon, she told him all that was on her mind. Solomon answered all her questions; there was nothing hidden from the king that he could not explain to her. When the queen of Sheba had observed all the wisdom of Solomon, the house that he had built, the food of his table, the seating of his officials, and the attendance of his servants, their clothing, his valets, and his burnt offerings that he offered at the house of [Yahweh], there was no more spirit in her.

So she said to the king, "The report was true that I heard in my own land of your accomplishments and of your wisdom, but I did not believe the reports until I came and my own eyes had seen it. Not even half had been told me; your wisdom and prosperity far surpass the report that I had heard. Happy are your wives! Happy are these your servants, who continually attend you and hear your wisdom! Blessed be [Yahweh] your God, who has delighted in you and set you on the throne of Israel! Because [Yahweh] loved Israel forever, [God] has made you king to execute justice and righteousness." Then she gave the king one hundred twenty talents of gold, a great quantity of spices, and precious stones; never again did spices come in such quantity as that which the queen of Sheba gave to King Solomon.—1 Kings 10:1–10

Participate in Your Own Rescue

When the queen of Sheba heard of the about the fame of Solomon, (fame due to the name of [Yahweh]), and his relation to the name of Yahweh, she came to test him with hard questions.—1 Kings 10:1

Do you know who you are? Do you really know who you are? And if you do, then why don't you act like it? As a poet has said, do you know that the blood of queens runs in your veins? Do you know genius is embedded in your genes? Do you know who you are?

Nations have leaped from your wombs, and while you raised those who have built kingdoms, you ruled and reigned as great wives, queens, queen mothers, queen warriors, and queens exercising authoritative leadership in your own right.

Do you know who you are? Ships have been launched at sea because of your beauty. Armies have gone to war. Swords have been unsheathed. Battle lines have been drawn. You have led the fight yourself, expertly strategizing with your admirals and your generals who bowed before no power but the divine. Do you know who you are?

You are a woman. And not just any woman, but you are a woman of African descent. Poets declare that you are the divine equal of man. You are daughters of the soil. You are born of the dust. You are sister, girlfriend, aunt, niece, granddaughter, and grandchild. You are wife, mother, and respected member of the family.

Do you know who you are? You are mother of the world. You are bearer of life. You have captured the imagination of the world. The Greeks and the Romans still have not gotten over you. They have immortalized your images on vases, bowls, and urns. They still speak of your legendary heroics. Do you know who you are?

Great women are listed in your genealogy. Minerva is an African princess who serves as a goddess of wisdom in Greek mythology. Do you know who you are? If you do, then why don't you act like it?

Iyanla Vanzant will remind you that you already have within yourself everything you need to succeed. There is the fearlessness of warriors in your genes and the wisdom of your grandmother is in the recesses of your mind, accessible through the spirit. Do you know who you are?

Marian Wright Edelman will remind you that you are righteous warriors. "You are moral guerrillas. You are workers and nitty-gritty doers. You are detail-tenders. You are long-distant runners. You are energetic-triers. You are risk-takers. You are sharers and you are team-players. You are organizers. You are mobilizers. You are servant leaders. You are spiritual."

Do you know who you are? If you do, then why don't you act like it? Maya Angelou will call you a phenomenal woman. A phenomenal woman are you! Camile Cosby will say that you are protectors of the family. You are annihilators of obstacles. You are a splendid rainbow of shades, from cream to caramel to honey to chocolate. You are respecters of life because life blooms in your body. You are resplendent with straight hair, resplendent with curly hair, resplendent with twisty hair, resplendent and brave.

Do you know who you are? If you do, then why don't you act like it? You have it going on in business and commerce. You are an activist and you are a pacifist.

Adam calls you, "Bone of my bones and flesh of my flesh" (Gen. 2:23). The psalmist declares that you are "fearfully and wonderfully made" (Ps. 139:14). The Wisdom writer says that you are "more precious than jewels" (Prov. 31:10). Jeremiah says God has known you before your mama and daddy met (Jer. 1:5). Before the sperm had a head-on collision with the egg, God formed you in your mother's womb. God poured into you your personality, your gifts, your skills, and your talents and called you into being. God formed you in the dust and called you into your very being. God has orchestrated your past and your present and your future.

You are created in the image of God (Gen. 1:27). You are daughter of the Most High. You are prophet, you are preacher, you are judge, you are sage, and you are scribe. You are child of the light; you are child of the elect. You are heirs of God. You are pilgrim, you are priest, and you are of the royal priesthood. You are a particular person. You are saint, you are sheep, and you are a servant of God. You are a vessel of honor.

Do you know who you are? If you do, then why don't you, for God's sake, please, act like it? You are a woman of African descent. Power is in your hand! You are a woman with the power to act, the power to do, and the power to produce. You have the power to listen as well as to speak up. You have the power to live honestly. You have the power for reciprocal trust and love. You have the power to share your joy, and the power not to not let racial or sexual obstacles get in your way. You have the power to be decisive and make timely choices. You have the power to change your mind. You have the power to be knowledgeable. If there is anything you don't know, you have the power to get it, study, research, and rehearse to get what you need to know. You have the power to give yourself a way as well as the power to receive from others.

You have the power to set goals and pursue them. You have the power to laugh and be connected.

You have the power to have an open mind. You have the power to have an open mind to new ideas even if they are not your own. You have the power to accept another's difference as well as accepting your own. You have the power to be flexible, that is, to bend and not break. You have the power to speak your mind. You have the power to broaden your horizon. You have the power to unstick yourself from anyplace you are stuck. You have the power to step over your limitations, and you have the power to start over again until you get it right. Because if at first you don't succeed, you try, try again.

Do you know who you are? You have the power to respect the past and honor the bridges built by your mothers and your fathers. You have the power to carry the wisdom of the elders in your heart. You have the power of self-definition because you do not want to be a female impersonator. A female impersonator is someone who lives by another's definition. You have the power to vote. If elected officers do not hold to their responsibilities, you have the power to vote them out. You have the power to be seen when ignored. You have the power to be heard above the crowd. You have the power to be taken seriously.

Do you know who you are? If you do, then why don't you act like it? Frederick Douglass in 1893 did not know who you were. He was the most visible and profound man of African descent in his time. The most famous black man of his era did not know who you were. Monroe Majors was writing a book about "Negro" women in 1893. He wrote a letter to Douglass and asked him to review the list of women he had selected to be included in the work. He wanted Douglass's suggestion of women that should be included. The writer gave Douglass his pick, asked him for his input in a letter that is preserved in the work of Jessie Carney Smith, *Powerful Black Women*. She writes that Douglass responded that he knew of no black women of importance. He knew of no "Negro" women in the era that could appreciably be called famous. In spite of what Frederick Douglass said, Majors went on to publish his pioneering work. But it amazes me that somehow Douglass had never heard of Harriet Tubman. Douglass had never heard of Sojourner Truth. Somehow the works of Phillis Wheatley had not risen to the surface. It seems that Douglass did not know who you were.

A while ago, there was an article in the *Baltimore Magazine* on the big brain and highlighted twenty-five men and women because of their intellect, achievements, and vision. There were four black men, several white men, several white women, and several Asians. But in the entire city of Baltimore, there was not one African American woman listed even though there are Ph.D.s, entrepreneurs, a college president, and college executive in the area. There is a female state's attorney and a female lieutenant governor. There are female publishers of major newspapers. There are judges and medical doctors, and yet the writers of the article could not find one woman of African descent because they did not know who she is. My sisters, if you don't know who you are, others are certainly are not going to find out.

Even in our sacred literature, in the church and synagogue, there have been times when the writers simply didn't know who we were. The Bible is filled with countless women who are unnamed. Their history is missing, significant genealogy is absent because the biblical writers did not know who the women were. Pertinent information that was given by others is missing and some women were reduced to shadow. Women have been reduced to liner notes in the margin.

We know that James and John were the sons of Zebedee. We know the background of Joshua, that he was the son of Nun. We know that Lazarus came from Bethany and had two sisters, Martha and Mary. We know that Aaron was a Levite, the brother of Moses and Miriam, the son of Amram.

But many women are just listed as women; some of them are listed by location—the widow of Zarephath, the widow of Nain, or the wise woman of Tekoa. There are some women who are listed by circumstance—the woman at the well, the woman with the issue of blood, or the woman caught in adultery. Some are simply listed as "woman" or "women," or as Luke calls them "others." Nameless personalities are included because they could not be excluded. Let me say that again: Nameless personalities are included because they could not be excluded. In other words, when male biblical writers tell the story, they cannot tell the story without them.

Too often, men try to tell the story without you. They may not get your name, may not get your resume, may not have your agenda, may not know where you came from and who your mama or daddy are, but they still cannot tell the story without talking about women. Even biblical writers had to include women, their significance to the Christ event and their role in the plan of salvation. Their role as instruments of the divine could not be ignored and one such nameless woman is the Queen of Sheba.

Her story is told in the context of 1 Kings 10. We find out from other literature that the Queen of Sheba was a Candace. A Candace was a woman of royal personage who ruled in the line of Ethiopian queens in the Meroic period, a thousand years before the birth of Christ and one thousand years after the birth of Christ. The literature names her as Makeda; the Arabs called her Belkis; in other words, no matter when the story is told, she has to be included—and it does not matter who is telling the story. Whether African, Arab, or Hebrew, girlfriend has to be in the number! Her fifty-year reign included a massive kingdom that extended beyond the Ethiopian borders. Her kingdom included Ethiopia, sections of Arabia, Syria, Armenia, and Upper Egypt. In other words, the Queen of Sheba was "bad!"

In order to understand what is happening in 1 Kings, we have to back up to 1 Kings 9 and look at the latter verses preceding our scope. In verses 26 through 28, we find these words:

> King Solomon built a fleet of ships at Ezion-geber, which is near Eloth on the shore of the Red Sea, in the land of Edom. Hiram sent his servants with the fleet, sailors who were familiar with the sea, together with the servants of Solomon. They went to Ophir, and imported from there four hundred twenty talents of gold, which they delivered to King Solomon.

Here, we find the impetus or motivation for her trip to see Solomon. The text reminds us that Solomon's fleet was in the Red Sea (Sea of Reeds), and if Solomon's fleet is in the Red Sea, that meant it would eventually come in contact with the territory ruled by the queen of Sheba.

Understand now, that she was going to see Solomon because Solomon's fleet was in her backyard. Everybody knows that when you start to mess with our backyards, we have to go find out what's going on. The two shared rival commercial interests: Solomon controlled the land and the queen of Sheba controlled the seas. Sheba would give Solomon an edge over land, but the seas were hers. In other words, she stayed out of his backyard, and he was supposed to stay out of her backyard. But since he came to her backyard, she had to find out what was going on. Solomon's fleet encroached on Sheba's influence, and so the queen of Sheba goes to visit, under the guise of going to test him with hard questions.

Sometimes, we don't always tell what's going on. We go around Robin Hood's barn. Wisdom was valued in this ancient time. Wisdom was valued to the point that heads of state would visit each other and exchange wisdom. They would test each other with hard questions to see who would come out on top. It was like playing Monopoly, Trivial Pursuit, or Jeopardy with one another. She went and asked him questions. The Word of God says that there was no question that he could not answer. The first three verses are just dry narration; she goes to see him, but Solomon is successful in expressing his wisdom.

The Queen of Sheba was impressed. The *New International* Version says she was "overwhelmed." She was overwhelmed by the impeccable dress of his servants, the house that he built, the palace that she found, the food that was on his table, the number of officials, the incense, and cupbearers. She was overwhelmed by the hospitality of the servants who served and the sacrifice that he offered daily in the Temple.

The King James Version puts it this way, "and the half has not been told."

In other words, she discovered that God was behind the rule of Solomon. God had blessed him and placed the kingdom in his hands. In response to what she found, the Word says that she left him and gave him gifts: a hundred and twenty talents of gold, precious stones, and spices which had never been seen before in Jerusalem.

Following her departure, legends followed the queen of Sheba. Legends sprang up all over the place that camouflaged and overshadowed the intent of her visit. Legend has it that the queen of Sheba heard there was a good-looking man in Jerusalem, and she had to go see him for herself. She went to see him, they fell in love, and they had a love child. This child, a son, began a Solomid line of Ethiopian rulers that continued until modern time. It is written in the Ethiopian constitution that Haile Selassie was the last of Solomon's line, dying in the 1950s.

But I declare to you, the girl was not sidetracked by legends and rumors. She was a woman who knew exactly who she was. You ask, how so? Women who know who they are, are women of purpose. Women who know who they are, do not wait—waiting for life to happen, waiting for a break to come, waiting for a move, waiting for a promotion, waiting for a job, waiting for a breakthrough, waiting for life to come along. Rather, they are women of purpose, not waiting for life to happen, but happening to life! All too often, sisters are waiting for something to come along: "I am waiting for that man to come along. When he comes along, everything will be all right. Life will be brighter. Life will be sweeter, everything will be all right."

If you haven't said it recently, you have said it sometime in your life: "As soon as I get my man, I will be all right. I don't have to pay these bills by myself. I have somebody else to lean on. I am going to find somebody to take care of me. I am tired of taking care of myself. I don't care what he looks like. I don't care what, as long as he is able to take care of me." Some women are sitting around waiting for life to happen: "As soon as I get a little bit of money, I am going to live. As soon as I get a little bit of a job, I am going to live. As soon as I get my little bit of promotion, I am going to live."

You spend all of your life sitting around waiting for something to happen. No! Women who know who they are, are women of purpose: "I know who I am and I know where I am going. I am not going to sit around floating in life until something happens. I know that I am complete in Jesus Christ."

The queen of Sheba did not leave the north of Africa just to go to the Fertile Crescent to have tea with the king in the palace because there was a good-looking man in Jerusalem. She had good-looking men in Africa. She did not have to go up there to find somebody else who looked good. Other scholars have noted that this queen was really on an official head-of-state visit. She was a woman of purpose. She left her home because Solomon had encroached on her backyard. She went there to be sure that she could establish trade routes to the east. After all, if Solomon is now in the sea, she ought to be in the desert. Fair is fair. She went there to sign treaties and for a safe passage agreement.

Other scholars have noted that the queen of Sheba went to Jerusalem to open up new markets for her goods and her services. She was on a peace mission to assure that war would not break out so she could continue her program to extend the borders of her kingdom. That is a woman of purpose. Women who know who they are will refuse to be sidetracked by frivolous, trivial, and minor things. Women who know who they are women of purpose.

If you know anything about football, you know that a coach teaches the halfbacks how to carry the ball. Now when the halfbacks carry the ball, they are taught to tuck the ball under the arm and to hold it at the tip. Then, they are to protect it while they run or if they fall. The coach will teach them to run leaning forward. This is different from how we usually run. In order to run leaning forward, you have to have purpose and be intentional about it. You just don't accidentally run leaning forward. We usually run upright. So, in order to run leaning forward, you have to do so on purpose. Why does the coach tell the halfbacks to run leaning forward? If they get tackled, they fall, gaining rather than losing yardage. That's a person of purpose.

Women, we are to live leaning forward because, if by chance we get tackled on the way, we will go down gaining rather than losing: "I didn't make a touchdown this time, but I'm a little further down the field than I was the last time. I am too far away to get a touchdown, but it looks like I am in field goal position." Now, the next time you are watching a football game with some men, you can say, "The coach teaches the players to run leaning forward!" Or you can say, "The player is really holding the ball well and that is just how he is supposed to hold it." Or, "That's why he fumbled, he wasn't holding the ball correctly. He didn't protect the ball with his hand!" You know, a little knowledge is a dangerous thing!

Do you know who you are? If you do, then why don't you act like it? Women who know who they are, don't get caught up in a "she-thing." Do you know what the "she-thing" is: "Where does *she* think she's going? What is *she* up to now? What does *she* think she is doing? Why is *she* here?" You see, we use the "she-thing" to keep each other in place. The moment a sister steps outside the place where we have placed her, we use the "she-thing" on her. We use it the moment a sister rises to prominence. We pigeonhole each other. We assign a places to one another: "Girl, this is your place and you stay right here. This is your place and we know where you are going to be! We are going to be right here and you are going to be right there."

We use the "she-thing" to keep one another in place. But the moment you make up your mind, you are going to win. You are going to lose that weight and you don't care what others say. You are going back to school and you don't care what others say. You are going to start your own business, and you don't care what others say. You are going to leave that job behind and move on to the next one. You are going to take that promotion even though you are not quite prepared for it. You are going to do some on-the-job training. You just let them *she* all they want: she, she, she, she! My mother used to say to me, "Every time you step outside, somebody always has a lot to say about you and what you do. You just step outside and go wherever God tells you to do. Let them holler all they want!"

If you have to use a "she-thing," turn to Proverbs 31:10–31. There is a whole lot of *she* stuff right in there: *She* is worth far more precious than jewels. *She* does good and not harm. *She* sets about her works with willing hands. *She* opens her arms to the poor. *She* is clothed in fine linen. *She* is clothed with dignity and strength. *She* speaks with wisdom. *She* laughs at days to come. According to verse 31, *she* gets the reward she has earned and her works bring praise. Now that is a "she-thing!"

Do you know who you are? If so, then why don't you act like it? Women, who know who they are, pass it on. Women who know who they are leave a legacy. Leave a legacy—make it so you can be tracked.

More recipes have been lost, more secret formulas are still secret, more wisdom has never been recorded, more knowledge has not been preserved because it all died with those who knew how to do it.

If you know how to do something, teach it. If you know what something is about, tell it. If you have been someplace before, tell somebody else. Otherwise, it will die with you. You can't sit along the sideline and say others ought to know what you know: "Shucks, we have been doing this a long time. We know how to do that." Then, why don't you go ahead and show others how to do that?

The excuses are not valid: "The committee did not invite me. I was not asked. I was not chosen. I am just going to sit back and watch them fall on their faces!"

No! No! No! If you know how to do something, get up and do it. But tell somebody else, too. The younger sisters in our churches or in our communities are dying and begging for the things we already know. You cannot say you don't know what to say to them— yes, you do! You knew enough to live to be twenty; you knew enough to live to thirty; you knew enough to live to forty; you knew enough to live to sixty. You have something you can teach somebody else. You knew enough to get a man; you knew enough to keep a man. You knew enough to keep your legs closed and your dress down and your mouth shut at the right time. You have to get up and tell somebody else. Women who know who they are, pass it on.

Women who know who they are participate in their own rescue. That is why I like this woman in 1 Kings. I like her because when Solomon's ships were in the sea, she didn't send advisers to scout it out. She was not content to sit at home and deal with second-hand information. She went to see for herself.

She participated in her own rescue. She did not wait for some mandate or a piece of legislature. She went to participate in her own rescue. She did not want a war. She did not want any encroachment on her kingdom. She did not want to fight about this. She went to dialogue with the king. In other words, she participated in her own rescue.

Do you know who Pat Riley is? He received an award from *Gentleman's Quarterly* magazine for looking good. He coaches the Miami Heat, a professional basketball team. My husband played basketball for about eight years. He and Pat Riley played on the same team at one time on the Portland Trailblazers. In his book *The Winner Within: A Life Plan for Team Players*, Pat Riley writes about the days when they had to "download." Professional basketball is a high-stress job. In order to be sane, the players have to step out of the fast lane and down shift, "download." So, they would do things together so that they could develop being team players and unload all of that stress. One of the things that they did was whitewater rafting. To me, this would be a high-stress process! Compared to playing professional ball, whitewater rafting is a low-stress process.

Pat Riley writes about the time that he went whitewater rafting. The guide laid out their equipment and explained to them what was going to happen. The guide made things very clear: "This is the paddle. Put the paddle in the water. Hold the paddle this way." The guide encouraged the men to follow his direction. He explained that there were rocks in the water and the players needed to wear helmets. The players had to wear wetsuits because, even though the weather was warm, the water would be ice cold. The wetsuit would protect their bodies and keep them nice and warm. Each man had to wear a life preserver. Although they could all swim, they needed a life preserver in case they fell overboard. The undercurrent and undertow would be very strong. One could be an English Channel swimmer and still get pulled under by the undertow.

If by chance a person went overboard, he must participate in his own his rescue. He could pop overboard and it would be too late to call the boat back. The others would be going downstream and they could not control the boat. The raft would go on, and the others might not know that anyone had gone overboard. Those in the raft would be going downstream and just a-paddling away. All of a sudden, someone is in the water! But the raft cannot back up to get you. Your screams may not be heard over the roar of the water. The man overboard must figure out a way to survive until he can be rescued.

Too often, we sit around waiting for somebody to rescue us. We say to ourselves, "If I sit here long enough, somebody will help me. If I will cry and have myself a pity party, somebody is going to remember me. Somebody is going to miss me. Somebody is going to call me in a minute to see how I am doing. Somebody is going to call to pray with me in a second. Let me see if I can reach my pastor and my pastor will pray with me. My pastor is going to give me a scripture to read that will make everything better."

Learn how to get down on your knees and pray for yourself. Open the Word for yourself. Get a Word from God on your own. Participate in your own rescue. Do whatever is necessary. You and God need to hook up so you can get out the mess that you are in. That is why I like the queen of Sheba. She participated in her own rescue.

Do you know who you are? Women who know who they are act like it! Sure, others talked about and gossiped about the queen of Sheba. Many did not get the story straight. No one has all of the facts, and scholars debate about who she is. Part of their observation is fact and part is legend. She, perhaps, was a legend in her own time, but that never stopped her from being who she was. She did not act as others wanted her to act. She did not interrupt her agenda. She did not change who she was. She just kept acting the only way she knew how.

If you know who you are, act as though you know! Stop trying to act like television and entertainment celebrities. You are a child of God. You are a woman created in the image of God. Stop lowering your standards to fit in or to get into certain circles. Set your sights straight on the vision; get yourself focused on where you need to be. Stop hanging around substandard people who are going nowhere. God has brought you to where you are right now; you are sharp, brilliant, bodacious, exquisite, and unique. You are intelligent., you have potential and possibility. You have a purpose, and you ought to act like it. You do not have to camouflage your femininity. You do not have to advertise your femininity. You are a woman of God, so act up! When folks come around and ask what is the matter with you, simply say, "I'm acting the way God created me to act. I'm doing what God created me to do. I'm going where God tells me to go, and if you don't like it, that's too bad. Like Esther, if I perish, I perish, but I am going to see the king."

Women who know who they are know God. The queen of Sheba knew that God was behind Solomon's power and status. This was not just a man's doing. This was not just a man's intellect or a man's organization. This was divine power at work. Women who know who they are know God. God put you together. God orchestrated your life. God designed you. God matched up your nose, your mouth, and your hair. God gave you your body and put it in right proportion. How can you know yourself if you do not know your Maker? How can you know yourself unless you know the one who put you together? Who knows better what you are like? God knows exactly what you need. Instead of walking around stating what you need or what you want, you had better check with God. Women who know who they are know God. They know that God's wisdom empowers their minds. God's intellect informs them. God's knowledge keeps them out of trouble. God's love digs them up out of the grave. God's mercy is brand new for them every morning.

You do not deserve God's grace and you cannot earn it. God gives it to you anyhow. Glory to God! It is God who stands with you. It is God who backs you up. It is God who walks with you everyday. So, when the world says "no," God says, "Go." When the world says "can't," God says, "Do." God gets you in when others shut you out. God sends you over everybody else and puts you in line. Women who know who they are know God. And if you know God, you need to act like it. Instead of walking around with your head down, body all bent over, dragging yourself from one place to another, getting all caught up in the role of victim, you need to turn to God. Do you know God? If you know God, stand up, square your shoulders, and lift your head. You are a queen. You are a child of the Sovereign. Straighten up your back and act as though you have royal blood. The Holy Spirit has imparted stuff to you that humankind cannot give you. Come on, act up! Make the devil a liar. The devil has a rumor out on you—says you are not going to make it,; that you are worthless,; that you are a nobody,; that you are not going anywhere in life. So, go ahead and act up! Make the devil a liar. Act up! Act up!

Others are going to accuse you of every bad thing they can think of. They are going to say that you are too aggressive. Tell them, "So what? I'm just acting up!" They are going to say that you are too assertive. Tell them, "So what? I'm acting up!" Some will say that you are out of your place. Tell them, "Yes, absolutely. I'm in the place where God has put me."

Women, do you know who you are? You have the blood of queens running in your veins. You have genius embedded in your genes. Do you know who you are? Creativity is in your consciousness. Do you know who you are? Victory is your middle name. Do you know who you are? Tenacity is the first word spoken by your gender. Do you know who you are? If you do, then act like it!

Women who know who they are women of purpose—they don't get caught up in the "she thing." Women who know who they are leave a legacy. Women who know who they are participate in their own rescue. Women who know who they are know God. I hope you will write this down in the bathroom or in the kitchen because those are the two places we visit often. Put these words where you can see them to remind yourself to be focused. Regardless of what anybody says, it is really what God says that counts. We are often so concerned about what others think that we never really check in with God to see what God thinks. God has created you. God can guide you and lead you. But the issue, my sisters, is do you know who you are? If so, then act like it!

Notes

ஃ

CHAPTER 1

1. Saran Eisen, "What's New?," *Marie Claire Magazine*, April 2001, 19.

2. Patricia Reid-Merritt, *Sister Power: How Phenomenal Black Women Are Rising to the Top* (New York: John Wiley & Sons, 1996), 27.

3. An extensive discussion on the definition of leadership is done in in my first book, *Not without a Struggle: Leadership Development for African American Women in Ministry* (Cleveland, Ohio: United Church Press, 1996), 64.

4. Walter Bennis and Burt Nanus, *Leaders: The Strategies for Taking Charge* (New York: Harper & Row, 1985), 4.

5. McKenzie, *Not without a Struggle*, 4.

6. Patricia Aburdene and John Naisbitt, *Megatrends for Women* (New York: Fawcett Columbine, 1993), xii.

7. Leighton Ford, *Transforming Leadership: Jesus' Way of Creating Visiion, Shaping Values, and Empowering Change* (Downers Grove, Ill.: InterVarsity Press, 1991), 25.

8. Ibid., 26.

9. John C. Maxwell, *The 21 Irrefutable Laws of Leadership. Follow Them and People Will follow You* (Nashville, Tenn.: Thomas Nelson Publishers, 1998), xx.

10. Bennis and Nanus, *Leaders*, 5.

CHAPTER 2

1. Veronica Duncanson was a part of a group of fifty women who responded to a "Strength in the Struggle" survey. The survey was sent to women from diverse fields including a state's attorney, an actress, doctors, an architect, ministers, laypersons, politicians, scientists, and business persons. Some of the responses are included in this work.

2. Patricia Aburdene and John Naisbitt, *Megatrends for Women* (New York: Fawcett Columbine, 1993), 98–99.

3. Ibid., 103.

4. James McGregor Burns discusses at length transactional leadership in his book, *Leadership* (Grand Rapids: Harper & Row, 1978), 257–397. He defines transactional leadership considered by some to be traditional male leadership (19) and transforming leadership (20). Transacting reflects male traditional leader behaviors while transforming reflects the characteristics often ascribed to women leader behaviors.

5. Aburdene and Naisbitt in *Megatrends for Women* gives a list of the characteristics of traditional management (100) which mirrors many of the characteristics that Burns lists in *Leadership*. They included relying on giving orders, limits and defines, and reaches up and down. These authors note that men tend to see job performance as a series of transactions (99).

6. Frankie Jacob Gillette responded to the "Strength in the Struggle" survey. In her responses, she included her resume and a copy of *It's Time,* a newsletter of the Time Savings and Loan Association (fall 1983). Mr. Gillette's comments were taken from that newsletter from a story about Ms. Gillette as a member of the Board.

7. Diane Cyr, "How To Do Everything: A CEO and Mother of Seven Makes It All Seem Very Simple," US Airways *Attaché Magazine,* January 1999, 38–39.

8. These comments from Rev. Camille Russell, as well as the comments from many of the women who follow, are from the "Strength in the Struggle" survey.

9. Patricia Reid-Merritt, *Sister Power: How Phenomenal Black Women Are Rising to the Top* (New York: John Wiley & Sons, 1996), 27.

CHAPTER 3

1. Susan Hill Lindley, *You Have Stept Out of Your Place: A History of Women and Religion in America* (Louisville, Ky.: Westminster John Knox, 1996), 173. Lindley indicates that it was slavery in the first half of the nineteenth century and continued racism after the Civil War that shaped the lives and religion of black women. Experiences with continued racism and sexism still have a profound affect upon women of African descent in the twenty-first century.

2. Cheryl L. McAfee, president of Charles F. McAfee Architects and Planners, is a respondent to the "Strength in the Struggle" survey.

CHAPTER 4

1. Phil Porter, *Eat or Be Eaten!: Jungle Warfare for the Master Corporate Politician* (Paramus, N.J.: Prentice Hall, 2000), viii. It is Porter's contention that management in the real world is rough and raw. It's where you are either the master chef or you are the meat cooked and served.

2. Ibid., viii.

3. From "Love Lifted Me," *A.M.E.C. Bicentennial Hymnal* (Nashville: The AME Church, 1986), 461.

CHAPTER 5

1. Patricia Reid-Merritt, *Sister Power: How Phenomenal Black Women Are Rising to the Top* (New York: John Wiley & Sons, 1996), 23.

2. From "There's Not a Friend Like the Lowly Jesus," *A.M.E.C. Bicentennial Hymnal* (Nashville: The AME Church, 1996), 381.

CHAPTER 6

1. Linda Phillips-Jones, *Mentors and Protégés* (New York: Arbor House, 1982).

2. James M. Kouzes and Barry Z. Posner, *The Leadership Challenge: How to Get Extraordinary Things Done in Organizations* (San Francisco: Jossey-Bass, 1989), 9.

Other Books from The Pilgrim Press

NOT WITHOUT A STRUGGLE
Leadership Development for African American Women in Ministry
VASHTI MURPHY MCKENZIE
Vashti Murphy McKenzie's best-selling book provides a historical, theological, and biblical overview of female leadership in the church. She suggests a model based on the "Woman Surviving in Ministry" project to promote an environment conducive to learning and dialogue among peers and mentors.
0-8298-1076-5/Paper/144 pages/$15.95

TAKING BACK MY YESTERDAYS
Lessons in Forgiving and Moving forward with Your Life
LINDA H. HOLLIES
"A must read book! Linda Hollies has successfully combined personal honesty and solid biblical storytelling to teach us how to forgive and let go of yesterday. . . . The prayers will inspire you. The principles will encourage you. The psalms will direct your path."
—Iyanla Vanzant, author of Acts of Faith
0-8298-1208-3/Paper/192 pages/$10.95

DAUGHTERS OF DIGNITY
African Women in the Bible and the Virtue of Black Womanhood
LAVERNE MCCAIN GILL
To reclaim a connection with their deep ethical roots and moral heritage, African American women must learn the stories of strength, courage, and faith. *Daughters of Dignity* seeks to identify these virtues and trace their roots. LaVerne McCain Gill provides suggestions for self-evaluation and narratives on contemporary programs to successfully reestablish an ethic of black womanhood in the community.
0-8298-1373-X/Paper/176 pages/$16.95

JESUS AND THOSE BODACIOUS WOMEN
Life Lessons from One Sister to Another
LINDA H. HOLLIES
Linda Hollies serves up new spins on the stories of biblical women. From Eve to Mary Magdalene, portraits of the bodaciousness of the many matriarchs of the Christian tradition will prove to be blessings for readers. Study questions and suggestions providing examples of how one can grow in faith, spirituality, and of courage—bodaciousness—are included at the end of each chapter.
0-8298-1246-6/Paper/224 pages/$11.95

MOTHER GOOSE MEETS A WOMAN CALLED WISDOM
A Short Course in the Art of Self-determination
LINDA H. HOLLIES
Fairy tales will never be the same! Linda Hollies retells classic fairy tales with a decidedly spiritual spin. She provides a guidebook for women at the crossroads of their lives while looking at biblical women. The result is a biblical approach to practicing the art of self-determination.

0-8298-1348-9/Cloth/142 pages/$21.95

MY MOTHER PRAYED FOR ME
Faith Journaling for African American Women
LAVERNE MCCAIN GILL
How do you develop the discipline of writing a faith journal? LaVerne McCain Gill provides guidance to African American women for writing and recording their spiritual witness. She begins by offering a five-step process for journaling, focusing on the stories of the Bible, and personal witness to the presence of God in contemporary life.

0-8298-1396-9/Cloth/104 pages/$14.95

STILL GROOVIN'
Affirmations for Women in the Second Half of Life
RUTH BECKFORD
Drawing on her own extraordinary range of experience in dance, theater, and community service, Ruth Beckford shows how life can and should be lived to the fullest. *Still Groovin'* touches on every aspect of women's lives—from health to empowerment to romance to inner piece. It is full of humor, insight, and wisdom.

0-8298-1337-3/Cloth/152 pages/$19.95

BAD GIRLS OF THE BIBLE
Exploring Women of Questionable Virtue
BARBARA J. ESSEX
Bad Girls of the Bible presents selected women of the Bible in a new light. Designed as a fourteen-week study, the book explores the Bible's accounts of traditionally misunderstood or despised women. Barbara Essex includes questions for reflection and provides helpful suggestions for ways to use this resource in preaching and teaching.

0-8298-1339-X/Paper/144 pages/$13.95

To order call 800.537.3394 · Fax 216.736.2206
Or visit our Web site at www.pilgrimpress.com
Prices do not include shipping and handling.
Prices subject to change without notice.